THE

LEADER

PARADOX

THE
LEADER
PARADOX

BUILDING HEALTHY TEAMS
AND SUCCESSFUL ORGANIZATIONS
THROUGH SERVING AND INFLUENCE

JEREMY GRAVES

Boise, Idaho

First printed in March 2023

Published by
JGG Coaching and Consultancy
3617 S Pheasant Tail Way
Boise, Idaho
www.jeremygraves.com

Editors: Kethjoy Watson, Zoe Simpson and Cameka "Ruth" Taylor
Layout by: BambuSparks Publishing
Cover Design: Olivia Prodesigns

For feedback, bulk orders, coaching, consulting or speaking engagements, contact the author at drjeremygraves@gmail.com

To my amazing wife, Stephanie
I would not be who I am today without your love and support.
Thank you!
To my son, Jordan,
I am so proud of your hard work and leadership in the classroom.
You are an incredible teacher.
To my son, Taylor
Your dedication and hard work in athletics demonstrates your leadership
on the lacrosse field.
Keep the net clear and lead on.

Foreword I

In reading the manuscript for *The Leader Paradox*, I was reminded of the reason I love working in leadership development. Jeremy and I share a passion for leadership that makes a difference. We are passionate about working with organisations to help them develop their leadership pipeline throughout their organisation.

I am a Leadership Specialist, author of PRIZE *Winning Leadership*, and I work with leaders of Not-JUST-for-Profit companies, but companies that are passionate about pursuing a purpose that is greater than simply making a profit. My mission is to "help difference makers make a difference"–a genuine, measurable, worthwhile difference.

Jeremy and I met at an online training and development event, where we were both studying to become certified by Patrick Lencioni and his team as Working Genius Facilitators. We very quickly recognised that we shared a love for Leadership Development.

The anecdotes, stories and thoughts that Jeremy brought to the discussion in the online workshop were both fascinating and insightful. His ideas were always relevant to the topics we were discussing. So, when Jeremy asked me to read his new book and consider writing a foreword, I was delighted.

Although the topic of servant leadership is not new, sadly, too often, it is the traditional hierarchical leadership model that prevails, especially in the VUCA season; a season marked by Volatility, Uncertainty, Complexity and Ambiguity, all at the same time.

Jeremy introduces the topic of servant leadership by discussing the five ways of being and the seven pillars of servant leadership. The heart of his discussion is centered around the core concept of a thriving culture, which ensures that everyone within the team is encouraged to flourish and grow, both personally and professionally. Team members get to feel valued for their contribution both inside and outside of their work environment. Each team member is given the right tools, training, education, and encouragement to make a contribution that helps them find personal meaning and value in their lives through their activities at work.

Jeremy shares some fabulous insights to help the reader understand the difference between a thriving culture and a burnout culture, and to see the importance of taking company culture beyond a few well-meaning statements in the business plan, or quotes on posters, into the everyday life of the organisation. He places emphasis on practicing your values, not simply professing them. Jeremy notes that a great way of understanding company culture is to understand how the staff feels on Sunday about going to work on Monday!

Jeremy's seven pillars of servant leadership provides a framework for every leader who wants to help the entire team improve their engagement at work and enhance their personal development journey. This inevitably results in a more committed and more productive workforce, who work together to achieve the purpose for which the organisation was created.

The Leader Paradox should be on the reading list for every leader and aspiring leader. It provides a great framework for leadership teams to work through together as they seek to pursue their purpose and make a difference in this increasingly challenging world.

Roger Fairhead
Author of PRIZE Winning Leadership

Foreword II

In *The Leader Paradox*, Dr. Jeremy Graves brings to light the importance of mindset and the value of putting people first as the heart of his message on leadership. He balances this perspective with the requisite skillset activities to put this principle into practice. The expertise with which Dr. Graves sheds light on the style and types of leadership, is breathed from the scholarly classroom to the everyday meeting of the needs of people in tangible and practical ways, and with a genuine touch of compassion.

In this book, Dr. Graves weaves the seven pillars of servant leadership in a way that is not a just a series of simple to-dos, and boom you are a servant leader. These are pillars that can help to shape a lifelong journey of practices that will evolve and grow throughout one's life.

I have had the pleasure of knowing Dr. Graves for about four years and witnessed his ability to lead in real-time, with people across various sectors. He has been essential in my growth as a leader and person. We met shortly after the passing of my father and his compassion during that time of grief was a comfort in a dark time. Through our friendship and professional interactions, I have gotten to see Dr. Graves' leadership in real-time, and I was honored when he asked me to write a foreword for him.

I have had the opportunity to serve as the inaugural director of the newly created Black/African American Cultural Center at the University of Idaho. I also have the privilege of being the father to my son, Malachi A. Graham-Pile, and through these joys, I am daily encouraged and challenged to grow as a leader. Dr. Graves would never say this about himself, but he is the embodiment of a servant leader.

I look forward to sharing this book with my students that are beginning their leadership journey and with those who have been leading for a while. I will encourage everyone I meet, who might even be slightly interested in the topic of leadership, to see the value of the servant leadership style.

Mario Pile
Director of the Black/African American Cultural Center
University of Idaho

Endorsements

As *author of over 40 books, I welcomed an opportunity to review what my friend, Dr. Graves, has carefully crafted in these pages on leadership. If you desire to have renewed passion for leading others from a strategic position of servant leadership, you will find a fresh approach in the wisdom of these pages. Learn how to thrive and empower others for a culture of growth for all. I highly recommend "The Leader Paradox."*

Gregory L. Jantz, PhD, C.E.D.S.
Founder, The Center • A Place of HOPE

Servant leadership is not a new concept and, therefore, it is often oversimplified. Here, Dr. Graves gives a clear analysis and explanation of servant leadership supported by his perspectives and from research about what it takes to be a servant leader in a practical fashion. It goes beyond simple definitions and provides examples and exercises to highlight the seven pillars of servant leadership. And he adds more richness with interviews from leaders using these pillars. This provides the reader with the depth and usable examples to start a journey to be a servant leader.

Dr. Francis Eberle
Senior Leadership and Organization Advisor

Contents

Introduction

Don't be impressed by degrees, titles, money, position or followers.
Instead, be impressed by care, concern, integrity, kindness and putting
others first. —Jeremy Graves

L eadership is about giving and less about getting. What if we as leaders served our teams instead of telling them what to do? Somewhere at the turn of the millennium, leadership ceased to be about controlling people. Business owners and executives discovered that caring for and about their staff made for better results. The traditional pep talks were seen for what they really were: lip service. Efforts were made to create a place where people could do good work and find meaning in it, causing them to bring *almost* their whole self to work.

In view of the pitfalls of traditional leadership, there is a need for a new leadership lens in many of today's organizations. I have studied the different types of leadership and taught a leadership class at Boise State University on "The Practice of Leadership." I recognized that too many organizations use a dictatorial or hierarchical approach to leadership. Far too many leaders do not develop their teams. Instead, they give the orders for their teams to execute and end up creating cultures that value processes over people. There is a need for a new leadership lens to help leaders effectively build healthy teams and successful organizations.

My terminal degree was in Transformational Leadership, and it involved the study of the different models of leadership. It is my opinion that the servant leadership model offers the best solution to the current leadership challenges in our postmodern workplace. This book highlights the pitfalls of traditional leadership and paints a picture of how to resolve these problems through the servant leadership model. The concept of servant leadership, though not new, is still foreign to the ordinary business environment. I believe this model of leadership is vital in transforming the culture within many organizations.

Servant leadership begins inward and flows outward. It is an *others first* type of leadership. In teaching on this model of leadership, this book takes you on a journey of self-discovery through seven pillars of servant leadership, providing explanations and activities conducted through real leadership training sessions in several organizations to help you to understand, appreciate, and practice these pillars.

I wanted this leadership book to be an easy read and as practical as possible. It will not only serve to improve your teams but will further your own development as a leader. The theme of care is greatly emphasized in this book. It is about creating a culture of care and service in our organizations. Those you lead and serve desire to know they are more than a cog in a wheel. As you develop your personal leadership skills, you will then learn how to share that journey with others within your organization, leading to a culture that embraces servant leadership.

You can be an effective leader by serving your team. This book provides examples of leaders across various sectors who are actually doing this and succeeding at it. The book shares their perspectives in what is called "the practitioner's perspective." If you desire to serve your team and help them become the best versions of their professional selves, pay heed to the seven pillars of servant leadership. The concepts presented will radically transform your organization as you seek to retain top talent and make a difference in today's world.

PART 1:
The Practice of Leadership

CHAPTER 1
The Pitfalls of Traditional Leadership

Fundamentally, the core of leadership is not about controlling people, but rather about caring for people. —Jeremy Graves

Eric breathes a long sigh and lets his pen clatter on the surface of his desk. How many times is he going to have the same conversation with his boss? James has to be the world's most overbearing and condescending boss. In this morning's meeting, he made fun of several team members to the point where one of them left in tears. Eric later discovered that that team member is actively looking for another job and I bet he's not the only one. Why can't James see how his poor treatment of the team directly relates to their desire to find work elsewhere? Eric wonders if it's worth having a conversation with his boss or is leaving the best option for him too.

Eric's friend from college works at an organization where they model mentorship and promote from within. They value connectedness and check in with their employees periodically. He boasts that the company operates with a sense of true care and concern for workers' wellbeing. Eric has even heard about how they allow for mental health days and actively encourage their team to take care of themselves. Their motto is "a healthy you is a healthy organization." Eric wonders if it's worth it to stay in a place where people are treated as mere numbers and not cared for beyond what they contribute to the company's balance sheet.

The Traditional Leadership Model

Eric's story perfectly illustrates the leadership paradox and the pitfalls of traditional leadership. Fundamentally, leadership is not about controlling people, but rather about caring for them. There's a big difference in our world today between leaders who attempt to control versus leaders who are looking for ways to care for their team.

If you go back into the research, most of our businesses are built on a top-down hierarchical leadership model; especially in the United States of America (USA). There are good reasons for this. This approach emerged out of a very militaristic background of veterans *cum* organization leaders in the post-war era of the mid-1900s. That was the way men in the workplace knew how to relate to authority figures. In this model, it is believed that those at the top think and those at the bottom do. Back then, the worker wasn't paid to think; he was meant to simply follow orders.

That became the general understanding for people just entering the workforce. They had to work their way up the corporate ladder, from blue collar to white collar. That idea of working your way up is still being taught in many of our business schools.

The problem with this traditional or hierarchical approach to leadership is two-fold:

1) **It often took decades for workers at the bottom to reach the C-suite.** They often experienced burnout or became disillusioned while climbing that corporate ladder because oftentimes, they have the solutions to fix or improve the processes or products stipulated by the

'thinkers' in leadership. However, they are either ignored or silenced. Can you imagine that Blackberry entry level worker who had been making suggestions for months, advising them to change to touchscreen technology?

2) **Only a small percentage of the team (the thinkers) is valued or prized.** It's truly a one-way dialogue and not a two-way conversation. As these traditionally run organizations fold, newer nimbler ones have noted their errors. They have adopted non-traditional and more inclusive leadership models. Microsoft, Apple, and Google are good examples of the deconstructed organizational chart in postmodern USA, right down to their black t-shirts and jeans in the C-suite. Everyone on their teams is expected to exceed personal and professional goals. Did you know Microsoft engineers are encouraged to create tools and register patents for their creations? That's forward thinking!

In the post-war era of the mid-1900s, this model was efficient but a poor way of leading any non-military organization. Hierarchical leadership is the way that many companies still function. I understand the importance of this within a militaristic setting. If I am in a battle, and the captain says throw the grenade, I don't think I should be asking why. Those are split-second life and death decisions. The majority of our corporate and manufacturing organizations today are not making life or death decisions.

For many of them, the more feedback from clients and employees they acquire and genuinely consider, the better business decisions they would make. Think of the humble loaf of bread in your home. When was the last time you had to slice it up yourself? Loaves came pre-sliced for the first time in 1928, after what must've been in hindsight, a pivotal sales meeting. In our culture, we have a saying for good things in our lives, 'it's the best thing since ... sliced bread!'

The problem is that today's leaders believe if they don't have the answers, they will be perceived as weak or inefficient. This is not an entirely false perception. Having all the right answers all the time is an impossibility, but that is the gold standard of a bygone and simpler era. This very hierarchical traditional approach has led to some of the current problems in the workplace such as dictatorial leaders. Those leaders who control the knowledge and information within an organization actually stifle their organization's growth in the process. These leaders hoard the information rather than share it and solicit feedback or suggestions.

The challenge with hierarchical leadership is that the leaders within such organizations are not actually thinking about employee welfare. These are the bosses who tell workers to quit their belly aching and be 'happy' they have a job. In the servant leadership model, which I will define shortly, the leader is thinking about serving those within the organization. The servant leader is seeking to empower them to share their voice in a way that gives them the freedom to be the best version of their professional selves. This is why the idea of servant leadership is a paradox and often evokes negative emotions.

The idea of serving and influence as a leadership model is about empowering those closest to the problems–those closest to the situations–to actually solve those problems. This is much like the Japanese philosophy of continuous improvement or Kaizen. It is a bottom-up style versus a top-down hierarchical style. As we distance ourselves from traditional leadership structures, I will introduce the seven pillars of servant leadership to be discussed in this book. These pillars cultivate healthy leadership practices in the workplace, empower teams, and will lead to the success of your organization. We'll discuss these pillars in more detail in Part II. First, let's look at the different types of leadership and why this book focuses primarily on servant leadership.

The Different Types of Leadership

There are several types of leadership models that one could employ to run an organization. None is more superior to the other. The leadership journey is about trial and error; seeing what fits your organization's needs to be successful. While studying leadership, it doesn't take long to realize that skills and traits have long since been a part of the discussion. What skills do successful leaders need to have? Are there certain traits that make a leader one that others emulate? Where do leader behaviors come into play as we discuss the leadership journey? These skills, traits, and behaviors, simply lay the groundwork for one to take a deep dive into leadership.

One can look at leadership through the lens of *transformational leadership*, where leaders seek to work on transforming organizations through teamwork and solving big systematic problems. *Authentic leaders* concentrate on passion, behavior, connectedness, consistency, and compassion. They ask questions about purpose, values, relationship, self-discipline, and heart. The *adaptive leader* looks at the big picture while listening to those closest to the problem for solutions in real time. These types of leadership along with *inclusive leadership* seek to ensure that everyone is a part of the conversation. All voices are accounted for in the problem-solving arena. These leaders are pre-occupied with the role of ethics in leadership, making ethical decisions (being good corporate citizens), and engaging with the world around them.

As I studied each of these leadership types, I realized that *servant leadership* encompassed pieces of all the types of leadership. For me, the servant leadership model is a conflation of several models. The transformational, since you serve your team thereby transforming your organization's culture. It includes authentic leadership because true servant leaders will operate from places of authenticity. They try to be the best version of themselves and inspire others to emulate them. It includes elements of adaptive leadership because it requires you to listen and focus on the importance of communication. The same could be said of *inclusive leadership* as you learn to include others and paint a picture that uses the strengths and talents of your whole team. Servant leadership borrows heavily from ethical leadership as it challenges you to lead with personal integrity.

I don't subscribe to ONE perfect leadership style; I have tried them all. I even have a doctorate designation in Transformational Leadership. But I come back time and again to servant leadership. It works for me because it encompasses many of the leadership styles that help me lead myself and others effectively, and perfectly captures the traits required for a good leader.

What Makes a Good Leader?

In conducting leadership training with different groups, I often ask the question, "What makes a good leader?" In our training, the participants work in groups to come up with a list of what they think comprises a good leader. Generally, the conversation flows around characteristics such as integrity, being good communicators, having clear goals, and focusing on the interest of individuals. After discussions about these traits, I would ask another question: "Are those characteristics just purely observed with your eyes or are those also things that you observed with your emotions?"

Good leaders are not simplistic; they observe with their eyes and their emotions. Yes, that's part of it. Their employees feel something when we are around them. We feel safe around them; we feel like we can be authentic—even trust them. Employees perceive that this leader does not only say they care but demonstrates it through deliberate actions. Do you have that inauthentic boss who greets you with a 'Hi, how are ya?' but never sticks around for your response?

Good leaders empower their teams; they don't take all the credit. Leadership isn't about holding on. It's actually about letting go. We tend to have this picture of leadership as controlling and holding on to territory. Rather, the good leader is making active plans to give up control. Does that sound counter intuitive to you?

I am part of a leadership team at Boise State University. Recently, the team I supervised worked on a very successful project. In the leadership meeting, my boss commended me. He said, "Jeremy, you did a great job." Immediately, I pointed out that it wasn't just me. the team worked hard on that project, and they should get the credit and ensured that the team got the recognition that they deserved. The team members weren't even in the meeting. It would have been so easy for me to just say, "Thank you very much." But I wanted the leadership team to know it was truly a group effort. In fact, I asked my boss' boss if he would send them a thank you email, and he did! It was an opportunity for the team to receive a few well-deserved pats on the back.

Good leadership is about thinking differently about how we engage with others. Building community is one of the most important attributes that leaders can bring into the workplace. It's more crucial to be *present* than to be the boss. Your presence is felt and appreciated as you involve yourself with what's going on with your team. It builds a sense of community in the workspace. This takes time, and deliberate intent, so you look for opportunities to invest in those team players who could propel the company and themselves to the next level.

One of the ways we build community and our team is by articulating what workers bring to the team, what you bring to the organization, and how you can both leverage that. At Boise State University, we have a little trophy that is passed around during our regular meetings. It is the responsibility of the last awardee to choose the next person who worked hard on a project that week, or who has gone above and beyond the call of duty. In this way, we are all looking for how each person is contributing to the success of the entire team.

At the base of the trophy are the words, "THE AWESOME AWARD. *Good work this week. You were awesomely awesome.*" It's a small gesture that cost me $10, but it sends a message that someone on the team this week worked hard, and it did not go unnoticed. The fun part is the person who wins the trophy proudly displays it at their desk for the week.

Leadership is more about giving than it is about getting. Leadership expert, Dr. John Maxwell, says, "Leadership is influence."

I believe the more influence you have, the less of yourself can be involved in that process. I think sometimes we think leadership is about a position, and once we arrive in that position, we now have the ability to control what everyone does.

The greatest leaders I've seen, the ones who truly have made an impact on my life, are the people who cared about me, and not simply exercised control over me. What does it look like for me to really begin to let go of my ego? It means looking for ways to engage with others around the topic of letting them be the best version of themselves when they show up for work. It's not about holding on to the territory and saying, "what can I get?" It's about letting go of my ego and saying what can I get out of my engagements with my team.

Recently, my team moved into a new shared office space for our entire team. This space has amazing windows and a great view. The problem is when we moved in, the windows were really dirty and we could not take advantage of the scenery. I was anxious to see the view of the Boise River and the green belt that overlooks it. On my day off, I came in and washed all the windows (not just mine) with the intent to say to our team, "Hey, look we have a gorgeous view here; I want to make sure that we take advantage of it."

This was a simple act of service that actively showed that I cared about the team's wellbeing; not just mine. It was also an act of community building. Yes, we could've have made it a group effort to wash the windows, but I was the one with the day off and good squeegee skills. The way to build teams is through letting go of what we think is going to make us great leaders.

Leadership is less concerned with pep talks and more concerned with creating a place in which people can do good work, find meaning in their work and bring their whole self to work. One of the ways we approach that in our organization (at Boise State University and consulting with teams in different organizations) is to remind them that we are whole people. As much as we would like to partition our various selves – our work persona and private persona, it is not really true. Think about it; the Jeremy Boise State gets on Monday after a horrible weekend is different from the one, they get on Friday, who can't wait for the weekend to begin.

Leadership ought to be concerned with how I engage with people and encourage them to bring as much of their whole self to work as possible. Again, this is one of the reasons I really believe in servant leadership because it addresses the whole person.

When conducting leadership training with teams, there is an activity we do called 'the human billboard.' I have done it with my team at the university, with several teams across the USA and other countries around the world; as far as India. I give people a large piece of flip chart paper. Then I ask, "Tell me about yourself using only pictures." Now for some people, that's very difficult because they often say, "I can't draw very well." My response to them is, "it is about their ability to tell the story of who they are and not about drawing me a masterpiece."

By giving people an opportunity to take some time to reflect on who they are and share their *billboards* with each another, we begin to understand that my colleague is not Mailroom Dan but a whole multi-faceted human being with passions, life experiences, quirks, talents, skills, and personality. This small activity is a way of reminding all of us that we are more than what we do for work.

As seasoned, aspiring or reluctant leaders, we seldom experience the many parts of Mailroom Dan or Stacy from Accounts. What are they passionate about outside of work? Do you even care? One of the ways you can find out is to go and spend some time with them at their desk. Look at their pictures, look at the way they decorate their desk, cubicle, or office. If you were to look at my desk right now, you would see several pictures that all represent stories about things I am passionate about. If you look just across the room, you will see that one of my co-workers has pictures of her family, and she will tell me about her family, if I ask.

So, what are your workers passionate about? What's their personality? What skills do they bring to the team? How do you help them leverage those skills? What about talents and upbringing? What about our upbringing? How does that impact how we show up and how we engage with others? Good leaders invest in and consider the whole. Oftentimes, leaders spend so much time in the workplace trying to make sure that our team does the work, that we actually miss out on the joy of the person sharing space with us. This kind of thinking, this awareness is built into the servant leadership model. I will expound in the coming chapters. Before I do, allow me to share my personal journey and how this model leads to healthier organizations.

CHAPTER 2
My Journey into Servant Leadership

Everybody can be great ... because anybody can serve. You don't need a college degree to serve. You only need a heart full of grace. And a soul generated by love. — Martin Luther King Jr.

I was drawn to servant leadership because of my upbringing and having a few leaders who modeled it at a young age. When I was 18 years old, I had a boss. Her name was Sharon. She demonstrated care for me when no one else seemed to notice me. I worked as a house attendant in a hotel called "The Red Lion Inn." I was the kind of guy who would show up for work, work hard and then go home.

Sharon took an interest in me and helped me, not only to grow and develop as an individual, but also as a leader. She was the first person to give me an opportunity to move up in the organization. So, I got very excited about learning from her because I could tell that she cared about me. In many ways, she was the first person to model this type of leadership for me, this idea of serving the person that is right in front of you and engaging with that person. This is the heart of being a servant leader.

Throughout my work life, I have had two or three other leaders who fit into this category. For me, it became my lens of viewing the world because of how these leaders influenced me and how they had engaged with me in the process. Since Sharon gave me that opportunity to grow at 18 years, I have been on quite a journey of learning about leadership. I thought I was going to be in the hotel industry because that's where I was working at the time. I thought, "surely, this will be my future."

However, a series of events led me to other places. I ended up moving into manufacturing and technology and eventually into a nonprofit space, where I began to do some work among people that were experiencing homelessness and housing insecurity. These activities led me into some of the leadership roles that I currently have, both at a community level and within the university. Although Sharon was really instrumental at the beginning of my leadership journey, there were a few other leaders along the way who spent time with me and helped me develop as a leader.

Along the journey, I realized that the key to leadership was this idea of servant leadership. It seemed like a "no brainer" but so few people were doing it. I found it fascinating; this idea of seeing a leader who cared about their subordinate and invested in that person. It could be argued that other leadership styles, such as trans-formational leadership and authentic leadership, also care about the whole person. I believe servant leadership embodies the boldest definition of caring for the person in front of you. I define servant leadership as:

> *Serving the whole person, the whole team, and the whole organization in such a way that people, teams and organizations move toward becoming the best version of themselves.*

I have observed people who poured into others. When that worker left their organization, it was viewed as a success because they helped them grow. They helped them move on to what was next. Other styles of leadership singularly focused on the bottom line, may view this as a 'loss of a valuable asset'. That is one of the reasons why some team members are bonded to their companies for a number of years after considerable investment of time and money has been made to improve their performance. Here's a starker outlook; unrealized ROI (Return on Investment).

On a more sinister note, their departure to 'greener pastures' might even sting the ego of the leader who loses him/her to the competition. Some leaders feel betrayed or used. Shockingly, leaders have hearts and feelings too. In a few cases, the reputation of the person may be tarnished by his former boss in a bid to make him unemployable. But that's in the extreme, not the norm.

Servant Leadership Modeled in Business

As a young adult, I did not have a name for it, but then I heard about this concept of servant leadership from a business leader named Robert Greenleaf. He was an AT & T executive who believed that the traditional leadership model was ineffective in truly leading people. Greenleaf felt the effects of it first-hand, as he had worked his way up in an organization. He then began to look at leadership through a different lens and in 1964, Greenleaf established the Greenleaf Institute.

In this landmark essay entitled, "The Servant as Leader" (1970) Greenleaf coined the term servant leadership and defined it this way:

The servant leader is servant first... It begins with the natural feeling that one wants to serve, to serve first. Then conscious choice brings one to aspire to lead. That person is sharply different from one who is a leader first, perhaps because of the need to assuage an unusual power drive or to acquire material possessions.

This definition captured my thinking and made me reflect on what kind of leader I wanted to be. In 1977, Greenleaf authored "Servant Leadership: A Journey into Legitimate Power and Greatness." In it, he talks about servant leaders who put other people's needs, aspirations, and interests above their own. I was hooked and my journey into servant leadership began.

When I found Greenleaf's work, I soaked it up and took it all in. I said to myself: "Yes, this is it!" Then I began to wrestle with the concept that servant leaders are deliberate in their choice to serve others first. This does not just happen naturally. They're very deliberate about how they do it—that they serve first and lead second was big for me. When I first saw this type of leadership, I thought to myself, "Wow! That's a very interesting paradox ... A leader's chief motive is to serve first as opposed to lead first." I continued studying Greenleaf and devoured more of his books and essays.

At the heart of Greenleaf's work is this concept that successful servant leaders will look for ways to serve their peers, their teams, and their organizations. He believed that leadership stems from servanthood and that truly great leaders will look to serve first. Upon his retirement from AT&T, he founded the Center for Applied Ethics, which eventually became the Robert K. Greenleaf Center for Servant Leadership, located in Indianapolis.

In doing my research, I came across another business leader who had written about servant leadership, James A. Autry. He wrote a book called, "The Servant Leader" and was the CEO of several magazines, including "Better Homes and Gardens." This was in the early 2000s. We can safely estimate that the span of application of this model in the workplace runs from the 1960s to the early 2000s.

Autry talks about what he calls "The Five Ways of Being," which he defines for the business community. I found his ideas fascinating because this is where I wanted to live. The translation of servant leadership into the business community was important for me.

The Five Ways of Being

Autry's Five Ways of Being are: *be authentic, be vulnerable, be accepting, be present, and be useful.* When working with teams, one of the things I like to do is to turn these into questions for themselves or their organizations. What does it mean to be authentic for you in the workplace? What does it mean to be vulnerable? Let me expound on each of these principles.

1). *Being Authentic:* According to Autry, being authentic means to be who you are. It is to be the same person in every circumstance, although your behavior may look different based on the circumstance. For example, how I am with my wife is different from how I am with my boss. However, it means I can hold myself to the same values and standards by being consistent with my values in my interaction with others, so that when I lay my head on the pillow at night, I know I am consistent with who I know myself to be. This is what it means to be the same person in every circumstance.

That way of thinking was priceless for me because it helped me to really understand that I can show up and be authentic wherever I am. I can be the same person no matter where I am within the organization.

2). *Being Vulnerable:* Even though our emotions are a crucial part of who we are, this is a dirty word in the workplace. Actually, it's more harmful to show no emotion than showing too much emotion. When Autry promotes honesty with the self in the context of your work, it's being open with your doubts, your fears, and your concerns about an idea. He takes it a step further by discussing how you can be open with your doubts, fears and concerns about employees' performance or about your own performance and be able to admit mistakes openly; admit you were wrong.

We adopted part of this into one of the organizations for which I was the Executive Director. We called it "Owning Your Oops." We helped people understand that it was okay to make mistakes. The worst thing you could do was to hide them. What we wanted to do was to bring them out into the open, to be aware of them so that we could talk about them and change as an organization. It started with me as a leader, being the first person to say I made a mistake, and then letting people know that we were going to be okay. When people made mistakes, we would work through them, and people weren't instantly fired.

3). *Being Accepting*: The idea of acceptance in our culture and in our day and age is massive because you are going to come into contact with people who think, believe, and act differently than you. How do we accept everybody on our team and help them know that what they say matters? It has to be according to how we engage with the team. According to Autry the ability to accept the ideas of others as valid discussions and reviews, focuses on the idea itself and not the person who presented them. Allow the ideas to steer the conversation and not the person who brought those ideas your way. For instance, supposed your working on a project around churn with your department. (Churn Rate is a sales term, meaning attrition rate or the rate at which customers stop doing business with a company). One person on the team believes the churn is the result of poor marketing. Another thinks it has to do with the pace at which product is being delivered to the customer. How do you listen to both sides and ensure that blame is not ascribed? If valid concerns are aired, you might just solve the problem of reducing churn and improving the Return on Investment (ROI).

4). *Being Present*: In framing it and bringing it into the 21st century, Autry was saying, "You have to be present." I realize that when I looked back at all of these leaders who have been influential in my life, the one thing that they had in common was that they were all present. They all showed up, they all listened. They put their phones down when I entered the room. They weren't distracted. Being present hinges on respect and respect will let any organization work like a well-oiled machine.

Being present is one of the most important things that we can do in leadership. It's being available yourself *or to yourself*, as you bring your values to bear on the work at hand, being available to others as you respond to the problems and challenges of colleagues, managers, employees and customers.

Being present is being in the moment, even in the hard stuff, and that's what I love about servant leadership. It has longevity because it's not just about where I can go and then move on. It's about being present with people in great times when they do great things and recognizing them in the hard times when things have gone off the rails. During the times, it would be easy to say, "You're fired" than to deal with them. I believe servant leadership allows us to sit with people in really difficult situations because we desire to be present.

5). *Being Useful*: What does the idea of being useful mean? To me, it is asking myself as a leader, "How can I help my team be the best version of themselves? What does it look like for me to help them as a resource? I like to think about the barriers I can remove for them to be successful. Sometimes that's actually helping them with training so that they get the tools that they need to be successful. Other times, it's being the person who removes a class barrier within the organization. Having the ability to talk with that person and helping to remove those perceived barriers can get their work done or move a project forward.

One of my editors shared her story as a middle manager at a bank. One cloudy morning, as she entered her office parking lot, she noticed her car window was stuck just as the rain came down. She pulled off to the side, got out, and tried to use her hands to force the window closed, but it didn't work. Other colleagues drove past, parked, and ran into the office as the rain poured, except a male executive, who stopped behind her.

Together, they tried unsuccessfully to close her stubborn car window. Then he suggested that she drive her car into his covered parking spot reserved for top tier C-suite executives. She did and after numerous tries, they both got the window closed. Up to this point, she was convinced that she was just a cog in the wheel of this company. His presence, honesty, spontaneity, very useful act of service restored her faith in the company and her purpose there. To her, in that moment, it was a kindness she desperately needed.

According to Autry, being useful is the most important thing that you can be as a leader. He recommends asking these questions:

- *How do I resource the people I serve?*
- *How will I help the people I lead be successful?*
- *What do they need from me as a leader?*
- *How can I help provide the tools they need to do their job?*
- *Do they need new equipment?*
- *Do workers need access to other parts of the organization?*
- *What are the resources that the teams need to be successful?*

These are questions I now ask on a daily basis as I think about resourcing our team to be successful. I have used Autry's suppositions and tweaked them somewhat in working with my team. On a daily basis, I think about how I can help my team to be the best version of themselves. Questions like:

- *What can I do to help our team and individuals be successful?*
- *What barriers can I help to move or remove so that they can be successful?*
- *How can I help elevate their voice within the organization so that they can be recognized and heard?*

As we take a deeper dive into the concept of servant leadership in Chapter 3, you will see how essential these *Five Ways of Being* are and why servant leadership has become my preferred leadership model to build healthy organizations.

CHAPTER 3
Building a Servant leader Organizational Culture

"The servant leader is servant first. It begins with the natural feeling that one wants to serve, to serve first. Then conscious choice brings one to aspire to lead."—Robert Greenleaf

B efore delving into the seven pillars of servant leadership and the characteristics of servant leaders, let's talk about culture. If we are honest, we have all experienced organizational cultures where we were seen as nothing more than a number. We felt uncared for, and sometimes not cared about—there is a difference. In these spaces, workers experience larger levels of burnout, serious illness, lower outputs at work, disengagement, more likely to seek work elsewhere.

A thriving culture allows those within your team to flourish and grow both personally and professionally. Thriving cultures get more work done, are more innovative, and employees simply enjoy their jobs. Figure 1.0 (p. 24) shows the impact of thriving vs. burnout cultures. As you know, the numbers don't lie. Thriving cultures can be established when servant leadership is evident.

Figure 1.0: Thriving vs. Burnout Cultures

What is Culture?

If the seven pillars of servant leadership are affected by culture, what is this culture? How does culture affect our team? What does that actually look like since we all have a culture? In this chapter, I will describe four types of culture which can be seen in organizations: *the stated culture, the shadow culture, the squirrel culture and the zombie culture.*

The Stated Culture

Everyone has a stated culture, which is often captured in the values by which the organization has decided it's going to operate and the values which the organization says are its priorities. Oftentimes, you'll see those value and/or mission statements on a wall, or on a business card, or on the back of a company badge that you use to get in and out of the building. Those values on the wall have buzzwords like integrity, passion, and purpose. We have all seen them and those values are important because they at least give us a starting point.

The reality is, it's the behaviors with those proposed values that actually create the culture because culture exists without you writing any of those words down. As a matter of fact, culture, many times, exists long before those words are actually penned, or before someone has been onboarded and has been through the process of learning what those words are supposed to mean. Culture is how your employees' hearts and stomachs feel Sunday night about going to work Monday morning. It's the feeling you have as you are getting ready to go to work every day. Culture is how the team actually responds to what the organization says about itself.

If you're *a numbers person*, think of it this way; culture is our values + our behaviors = our culture. So, the question is, how do you take those values and actually express them in behaviors? Think about your organization. Think about your values, maybe even stop reading right now, and peruse your company website. Look through the information that you have about your organization and see what your values are, and then ask, "how do my behaviors align with those values?" Moreover, what behaviors would I actually look for to say that a person is exhibiting those values? **Remember, it's our values plus our behaviors that equals our culture**.

The Shadow Culture

In many organizations, we have a culture that's stated and then we have the shadow culture. You may not have actually used those words, but you know exactly what I mean when I say *the shadow culture*. It is the culture that happens when the leadership is not around. For example, we have a stated culture that says care and concern about others, but then our shadow culture is selfish and self-serving. It is incongruent with the words on the wall or the website! I've heard people say that culture is actually the way things get done around here.

Our shadow culture is oftentimes more powerful than the stated culture within an organization. The shadow culture says, "when the boss isn't around, these are the corners that we cut. These are the ways in which we really do things." We are supposed to operate with this value, but in reality, this is the way that we actually operate. Those behaviors emerge in negative or unhealthy ways.

The Squirrel Culture

The Squirrel culture is a phenomenon that can be detrimental to organizational success. It occurs when individuals within a team or organization hoard knowledge or talents, refusing to share information or collaborate with others. Instead, they prioritize their own interests and protect their position at all costs. This type of behavior can create silos within an organization, hindering communication and collaboration between different teams and departments. It can also lead to a lack of trust and respect among colleagues, which can ultimately harm productivity and morale.

The Squirrel culture can be difficult to address, as individuals who exhibit this behavior may not even realize they are doing so. However, it is important for organizations to establish a culture of openness and collaboration, where individuals are encouraged to share their knowledge and skills with others. This can be achieved through training programs, team-building activities, and leadership that promotes transparency and cooperation. By fostering a culture of sharing and collaboration, organizations can avoid the negative consequences of Squirrel culture and achieve greater success as a team.

This leads to the final type of culture, and this is the dangerous one, the *zombie culture.*

The Zombie Culture

The *zombie culture* is when workers are walking around alive because they're living human beings, but they're dead to the organization. They are numb to the organization because they don't trust the culture. The culture is unhealthy, or worse, toxic. They are slowly limping along trying to figure out how to or if they should engage with the culture because they don't believe in it.

There is an ominous ending to the personal story my editor shared, which is a good example of zombie culture. After helping her fix her car window, the executive hurried inside the building. She then backed out of his covered parking spot and found a spot in the general area, then went inside. As she entered the office, she was summoned by her boss who scolded her (1) being late (2) having the audacity to park in the C-suite parking space (3) questioned who she thought she was. Her boss scolded her loudly, and she was embarrassed. She knew from past experience, it made no sense trying to explain the chain of events in the moment. Instead, she planned and executed a departure from the company. For her, that was a pivotal moment. Later that day, she quietly explained in detail, to her boss, the events that led to what she falsely perceived to be gross insubordination on her part. My editor received no apology or contrition.

Diagnosing the True Organizational Culture

When I'm working with teams, sometimes, I will ask, especially the leadership, "Can I spend some time with the people within your organization without you being around?" I'm only going to ask a couple questions, but I can get a real feel for the culture quickly. There are two questions that I ask. The first set of questions I'll ask is, "Do you enjoy your job? Do you enjoy working here? What do you enjoy about working here?" Sometimes I ask some variation of those questions and then I'll just listen. Then the second set of questions I'll ask is, "Would you recommend this job to your sister, brother, mom, dad, aunt, uncle, best friend, or cousin?"

You will learn a lot about the culture of an organization with these questions. Would you want others that you know to work there? Would that be a place that you want them to spend time, with which you want them to be involved? I will challenge people to think about their culture and I'll have them tell me what their stated culture is. Some can articulate their company's shadow culture. Then I would ask, "What about the zombie culture or the squirrel culture?" Do you see any of that beginning to linger or affect how you see the world?

Leaders, if we're going to be able to build an organization that has these seven pillars of servant leadership, we must start with the foundation: its culture. We must put some strategy around that culture to be able to effectively lay that out. Let me tell you this, sometimes we go into organizations, and we actually have to help with restructuring or repurposing the culture. We help people to really get to the core of what their organizational culture really is or ought to be.

Typically, it was a group of people, sometimes long before you came to the organization, that went away on a retreat and said, "these are going to be our guiding principles, and this is going to be our culture." When they returned, they gave the rank-and-file members the cliff notes (highlights) of the retreat. This usually comes with a prepared statement of the decisions on policy that inform organizational culture. Imagine all this happening two or three decades ago.

The problem with that is if your employees have not been invited into that conversation, it's not going to help anybody, and it won't be effective in actually creating a culture that is going to be meaningful to all your employees. The team will not buy what you're trying to sell them.

One of the greatest ways that you can help employees buy into your organizational culture is by letting them be a part of the conversation about the words that you choose. Once you have chosen the words, ask the team to help you with behaviors. For example, what does that look like if we're going to actually demonstrate that value within our organization?

Recently, I discussed this with a team that was in the process of a leadership transfer, the changing of the old guard, so to speak. Their leader that had been there for many years was getting ready to retire, and new leadership was coming in. The company went through a process of reviewing their values and asking the employees to give feedback on the following:

a. *Are these values still the values that our organization adheres to? If so, how. If not, why not?*

b. *If we need new values, what values should we be focusing on?*

c. *How do you see those values in the behaviors of people who are part of our team or a part of our organization?*

Culture becomes the underlying theme to successfully implement the seven pillars of servant leadership. Along with this comes the strategy to be able to do it. You can't reverse that. Oftentimes, people will start with strategy and want to build a culture around it. The problem is, you already have an existing culture when two people get together, let alone 4, 10, or 100. You will have people who will seek to move to the top and into leadership. You will have people who will seek to help influence that in both positive and negative ways. Have you ever seen an old gum ball machine? Something must change (inserting a coin) to start the mechanism inside to give you a gumball. There is a fair amount of jostling to be picked but a series of mechanism must align before a gumball appears. After all of that, it might not even be your favorite color; it's a gum ball, nonetheless. Always start with culture; culture is the base at which everything else is built.

If you want to change your office culture, it takes strategy. If you want to move towards being more servant- leader, shift the mindset about how you engage with others. If you want to work on how to develop an organization where people can grow and breathe and be the best version of themselves, start with yourself. Know what the current culture is and where the gaps are between your personal culture and where you want it to be. That's where the strategy comes in, because culture is ever changing. You ever wonder why a newbie is never asked to show another newbie around? The person who will "show you how things are done around here" is always the team member with experience and a fair number of years of service. Oftentimes, that person is loyal, commands the respect of not only peers but also senior team members as well. Culture is learned behavior and that takes time. Culture will determine how you grow your organization or cause it to fall apart. Side note: if you start losing the respect of your loyal team members, watch out!

Strategy is the way you can develop an organization that thinks about things ahead of a crisis like personal integrity and ethics, putting others first, collaborating, communicating and listening well, continuous team development, and leading with the future in mind. Do you really want to be that reactive leader who implements a strategy *after* an incident occurs in your company?

Introduction to the Seven Pillars of Servant Leadership

As we introduce the seven pillars of servant leadership and the characteristics of servant leaders, begin to do some self-examination. Ask yourself if you already possess any of these qualities. If not, what will you do to acquire these qualities. The seven pillars of servant leadership are:

1. *Personal Integrity/ Behaving Ethically*
2. *Others First*
3. *Communicates Effectively and Listens Well*
4. *Collaboration*
5. *Leads with the Future in Mind*

6. *Self-Care and Mental Health*

7. *Continuous Team Development*

The seven pillars start from within, then flow outward. You must have integrity and behave ethically before you can put others first. Putting others first starts inward with a decision and moves out with action to actually communicate with purpose and listen well, which leads to collaboration and looking toward the future, through thinking about things like caring for yourself and the team you are leading and continuing to develop them.

Each of these pillars exemplifies the characteristics of servant leaders as described by Greenleaf and Autry. Unlike other dia-grammatic representations of leadership pillars, each of my pillars is uneven. This suggests that leaders themselves have their own shortcomings. For instance, if you are naturally bad at communicating, your pillar would appear shorter than the other traits which you may be more adept at. I interpret that 'deficiency' to mean it is something you should be mindful of and seek the necessary support (see how many bricks are under the shortest pillar) to ensure the stability of your company. Here's a relatable example from the characters on the popular series, "The Good Doctor." Dr. Glassman is the old sage mentor of Dr. Shaun Murphy, a gifted young surgeon with Autism Spectrum Disorder (ASD) who has the most terrible bedside manners. However, because of his disorder, his capacity to diagnose and treat patients makes him an invaluable member of the team of elite surgeons. For Dr. Murphy, Glassman is his key foundation stone, along with other main characters.

Who is your Dr. Glassman? Are you even aware of your shortcomings? At this juncture, you may have realized that being a servant leader requires less hubris and more humility. Identifying your faults and asking for the support you will need will make you a more effective and authentic leader.

According to Greenleaf, these are the eight characteristics of servant leaders. They:

- *Put other people's needs, aspirations and interest above their own.*
- *Make a deliberate choice to serve others.*
- *Serve first, then lead.*
- *Serve the needs of the organization.*
- *Focus on those they lead.*
- *Coach others and encourage their self-expression.*
- *Facilitate personal growth in all who work with them.*
- *Listen and build a sense of community.*

When we talk about servant leadership in that paradox of service and influence, and contrast that with James Autry's five ways of being, there are several things that begin to emerge about the characteristics of a servant leader; their level of introspection; consistently looking for ways to grow themselves. I believe that good servant leaders are focused on what's happening within them. They have a high degree of self-awareness.

I believe *servant leaders are folks who first begin with inward growth and development.* This concept has taken on practical applications for me (personally) and has been taking me on different journeys along the way. If you are committed to servant leadership, you will be examining your own mental health and journaling in the mornings as well. This brings me to the 'v' word again—vulnerability. When Autry and Greenleaf championed vulnerability, it was a hard sell back then. Thankfully, in our post-modern society, it's no longer a bad word. Leaders from the traditional leadership model will struggle with being vulnerable and doing introspection. They are the ones who may be accused of being tone deaf, insensitive, or out of touch. Those leaders hardened against the emotive, must do the personal work to stay relevant and relatable to their team.

In my quest to grow and develop as a leader, I use different assessments and tools in a way that can be helpful in the process.

The second thing is, *servant leaders live by a set of values.* I'm amazed at how many people I've had the opportunity to work with who have not actually stopped and thought about what their personal values are. So, what is that true north for you? How are you showing up and engaging with your team? Medical professionals are guided by the principles of the Hippocratic oath. Teachers, lawyers and accountants all have professional bodies that ensure they tow the line. Why is it corporate leaders don't adhere to a "Do No Harm" policy too?

Guiding Principles/Values Activity

There is an activity that I do when I'm working with leaders. I give them a set of 40 different values. Now, we know that's not an exhaustive list, but it gets them thinking. I will have them lay all the value cards face up. They would then choose the ten most important values to them. Then we have a discussion about their thought process when choosing those ten cards. For some leaders, it's easy.

For others, this is a very laborious exercise to actually get through. Then I tell them to pick the five most important values from the ten. Now, this is where you start to see people slowly dig into certain areas and explain their choices. I've heard justifications like, "Oh well, this value is similar to this one, so I can put the two of them together. Things get really hairy when I instruct them to pick their 3 most important values from the 5. At this juncture, I ask the leader to share with their pairs why they chose those three. The pairs, in turn will articulate whether they see those three values lived out in their daily interaction with others in the workplace. I hope your talk matches your walk at this point.

Finally, I invite them to move from three core values to one. I tell them, "If you could live by only one value for the next 30 days, what would that value be, and why did you choose that one? It's a fascinating conversation because I think it's important for us as leaders, especially servant leaders, to always be thinking about the set of values that guide us. They will start to build corporate kingdoms as your reputation as a good leader spread. You could start to get a big head just in time for the next lesson.

Thirdly, *servant leaders share the credit*. Former US President Ronald Reagan used to have on his desk this saying, "there's no limit to what a man can do or where he can go, if he doesn't mind who gets the credit." True servant leaders are people who share the glory. An executive gave an assistant manager in her department a task to increase company profits. She succeeds and draws the attention of her boss' boss. Her smarts did not go unnoticed by the executive as well. After commending the assistant manager for her good work, she advises her, "The successes are mine and the failures are yours." Let me hasten to say this is the antithesis of the traits of a servant leader or anyone with decency, for that matter.

The last characteristic of a servant leader that I believe is really important is that *servant leaders know how to clarify vision*. They know how to take a vision that is a company-wide vision and bring clarity to it so that those within the organization feel that they know exactly where they're going, and how we are going to get there. In clarifying vision, A true servant leader will take the time necessary to paint that picture for those that are a part of their team so that there is a sense of clear direction, clear movement and clarity that is truly second to none.

Oftentimes we struggle in our organizations because they have lost their vision, or it's shared with a select few. Yes, the vision statement is hanging conspicuously on a wall. People recite the guiding principles or goals, but they are not clear every single day when they show up for work, Monday through to Friday. They are so connected to it that they can see it without having to squint or without trying to figure out how what they do connects to the vision of the organization.

It takes as long as it takes to acquire and manifest all four traits of a true servant leader. Errors will be made, losses conceded, and triumphs celebrated as a team. There is a famous saying that *there is no 'I' in team.* But there is 'Me' and that is not a bad thing, especially in the corporate world. Every good team must have a good leader. That could be you! As you self-assess, bear these principles in mind as we move into Part II of this book. It was important to share these characteristics as the backdrop of the seven pillars of servant leadership, which will be discussed next. In part II of this book, you will learn about each of the seven pillars of servant leadership and their applicability to the workplace. Interviews will be done with leaders in organizations which embody each of these pillars. Their input will be described as the practitioner's perspective.

These perspectives come from interviews conducted in 2022 with organizational leaders in different fields. It is my hope that this approach, along with the practical activities around each pillar, will help you to develop a servant leader culture within your organization, so that your teams will thrive, and ultimately, your organization will be successful.

PART II

The Seven Pillars of Servant Leadership

CHAPTER 4
Pillar 1: Personal Integrity and Ethics

"We must adjust to changing times and still hold to unchanging principles."—Jimmy Carter

Since servant leadership always starts inward and works its way outward, inward growth and development become very important and this ties in well with the pillar of personal integrity and ethics. This is the main pillar. Showing up without doing the foundational work will cause your company to be compromised. It's going to turn up in different ways, so you should be aware or be mindful of this pillar.

In my quiet time, I think of personal integrity and ethics through the lens of how I choose to show up for others and what that looks like. This pillar, personal integrity and ethics, allows us to have an operating system for engaging with others. It is being the best, honest, and most authentic version of yourself. It means no secrets. It is living in a way that your life is consistent in all areas—all the time. There's a paradox for you! Wouldn't it be absurd if you were only your best self at work and nowhere else? A person cannot be simultaneously bogus and full of integrity; that's the stuff of madness. And yet, millions of C-suite leaders try to pull this off with devastating results. This elite group of people will be the first to share the perks of the C-suite as well as the pitfalls. They are well acquainted with divorce, unhealthy personal relationships, mental and physical health problems. Take your pick. I suppose that's where the phrase 'married to the job' came from. What a tragic locution.

The root word for integrity is to integrate. This idea is that every part of my life is fused into the other parts so that there are no secrets in the way I live, publicly or privately. Many people struggle with authenticity. Which is the true self? Can you be a good servant leader *and* a good spouse/parent/sibling? Do you know that we inwardly start to crumble because we know that we are not being our genuine selves? It is painful to co-exist with liars, but that person is you ....

Ethics comes from following universal and timeless principle. These principles include honesty and integrity, treating people with respect, knowing right and wrong and the like. This is what behaving ethically is all about. A leader who embodies personal ethics and integrity sets clear and firm, yet flexible, boundaries. It is a leader who accepts and delegates responsibilities. It's a leader who shares power and control and helps create a culture of accountability, starting with themselves.

I love Brené Brown, a professor, lecturer, author, and podcast host, who has done some amazing work around the idea of shame, vulnerability (emotional risk), and integrity. She says that personal integrity is about choosing courage over comfort. Professor Brown talks about doing what's right over just what is fun. At the end of the day, it is our responsibility to do the right thing. Personal integrity is about doing the right thing. In *Dare to Lead*, she speaks of practicing your values and not just professing them. This concept is powerful, *practicing your values, not simply professing them*. This is an important distinction for us when we think about integrity and ethics.

At the end of the day, leading staff, family, or own lives is a full-time job. Sometimes we're doing a good job and we're displaying a high level of personal integrity and ethics. Other times, it is simply not our best days. Just remember, life is about all the little wins, not just the major ones. Leadership starts from within or as leadership expert Dr. J. Robert Clinton (2017) notes in his book, *The Making of a Leader*, "Leadership flows from being." It's as much who you are and what you do, not just your title.

It is like having an Internal Operating System (IOS). Your operating system is the way you see the world. So, how does yours affect your perception of the world? How does that operating system affect you when you are faced with ethical dilemmas? These include how we think about certain situations in the workplace, what do we do with information that we have been given and pass it along to others.

We will be faced with ethical dilemmas when a boss says, "Oh, just change the numbers ... just here just a bit; it's not going to be that big of a deal." We will be faced with ethical dilemmas when someone confides in you about something that they may have done that may have legal consequences for them. So, what do you do then, as a servant leader? It all boils down to your own IOS. Much like a duck on water, a significant part of leadership happens beneath the surface.

Enemies of Personal Ethics and Integrity

When you look at each of these pillars, each one has a natural enemy. When working with teams, I share with them the enemy that I use when I'm describing it to others, but then I would challenge them to think about what their enemy would be in their context. I am challenging you with the same thing. What would be your enemy? What would be the enemy of personal integrity and ethics for you?

A very simple enemy of these pillars would be not being true to oneself. Theoretically, people put on a mask and pretend to be somebody that they are not. These days, the 'fake it to make it' ideology is popular and dangerous. We are told of the success stories but seldom ever of the failures; and there are many. Even among those who successfully fool everyone, they live with the crippling fear of being found out (discovered) as a fraud. I suppose you can't fool yourself. So, is that authentic success if you are a financial and/or professional darling in the eyes of your peers and colleagues but psychologically, a mess? Conjuring ways to inflate or overextend our ego in a situation, can cause persons to perform contrary to their personal integrity or ethical decision making. As you begin to unpack your own life, what would be the enemy of your personal integrity and ethics for you? Think of these as your roots or foundations.

It has been said that truly behaving ethically is all black and white until you actually have to make a decision. We always live in that place of cognitively knowing something is right or wrong until we are forced to pick a side. Then we realize it is not quite as easy as we think. This is why people prefer to live in that foggy murky gray area, where we rationalize and make justifications. Personal integrity says these are my values; these are my non-negotiables; this is the internal operating system that I'm living under and through; this is how I choose to engage with others and to see the world. When we live by a personal set of values that begins to come out; when we don't have those values, we don't have a lens for making decisions, and we begin to get a little shaky.

Personal integrity and ethics also mean that we live from a prominent place of self-awareness. You purposely regard those with whom you interact with daily. Your actions are deliberate, organic and there's a consistency that's built into all of this. As I think about others, that helps me endure hardships well because we will go through hard times. When we experience hard times, that's when our ethics and personal integrity are tested the most. A servant leader is one who lives by a set of values and is a person of integrity; one who thinks about others and behaves ethically.

Personal Integrity and Ethics Activities

There are some great activities that you can do around ethics and personal integrity. One of my favorites is using an ethics ball that we throw around the room and have people actually answer the questions on the ball. There are all sorts of questions on that ball, and we use these questions to lead our discussions. For example, "Is it ever right to tell a white lie? Do you believe in the phrase, "finders keepers, losers weepers?" We discuss making those ethical decisions, and what that looks like as we walk this out.

Another activity we do is called the X, Y game, so aptly named because its roots lie in Applied Mathematics; Game Theory to be more precise. You may be more familiar with the Prisoner's Dilemma (PD) from your AP classes or college philosophy. Officers placed two prisoners in separate holding cells in an attempt to get one of them to confess. The officer introduces a white lie saying, "The other prisoner said it was your fault." Another officer goes to the prisoner and repeats the same lie. What you are trying to do is to get them to turn on each other. When we do this X-Y game, we put people in groups, and they have to hold their X or Y and there is a dollar amount attached to their X or Y.

The best way for everyone to win is for four teams to hold up their Y, but if three teams hold up a Y, and one team holds an X, then all the people who hold up Y get a negative one dollar. The teams who hold up X get plus three dollars, so you can see how people will start to turn on each other even in a game setting. This gives us space to discuss personal integrity and ethics in the workplace and what it really looks like for us to engage with others, and think about not throwing an X when we are connecting two people that are part of our team, but actually allowing everyone to throw a Y.

We have actually had companies that will use the XY terminology by saying, "Okay, we made a decision. Let's not throw an X. Let's all throw Y and let's be faithful to that decision." It is not always easy. It's actually difficult to dig deep into oneself at times and discover who you really are at your core. The first pillar (personal integrity and ethics) is the most important one needed to serve and influence anyone in your charge as a servant leader.

THE PRACTITIONER'S PERSPECTIVE

PILLAR 1:
PERSONAL INTEGRITY AND ETHICS

DAN DECLOSS
CEO and Founder of PlexTrac

Practitioner's Profile and Their Organization

Dan DeCloss is the CEO and founder of PlexTrac, a cybersecurity software company that supports security teams. PlexTrac sells software to security teams to help them automate reporting and tracking of vulnerabilities.

Question: What are your thoughts on personal integrity and behaving ethically?

I believe ethics is incredibly vital for a leader to be a good leader, and for businesses to be good businesses. For me, personal integrity is shaped. It's a part of who you are. It's your character. I define it as doing the right thing even when nobody's watching. This character is not just within your job, it's all of life. It also includes how you are interacting with society and the world.

In terms of the role both play in my decision-making and how they translate down into our organization, this is one of those issues where you have to practice what you preach. You must model it as a leader.

When a situation arises where integrity and ethics are tested, be determined to say, "Hey, we're going to do the right thing at all costs," even when things may not always be clear.

The team may ask, "what is the right thing to do here, collectively as a group?" Let them know we're going to put integrity above all else, in all situations" We are not putting profit or a buck at the top.

I model this pillar in how I run meetings and how we approach decision-making, and then I try to encourage and share that vision with the entire company. For me, integrity and accountability are two of my core values. They are also core in our company. These core values are not aspirational, we choose to live by them and that's how we've achieved what we have. They are also vitally important to where we are going and how we'll get there.

Question: How do you know if you are hitting the mark? Do you have check-ins or ways to see if people are doing so?

That's a good question. After a meeting, we don't necessarily say things like, 'How did you model integrity today?' But we do try to recognize when people have done a good job reflecting or adhering to our core values.

It's particularly how we treat people. I think that's an important part. For example, on sales calls, we check in and make sure we're not telling customers things that we don't do or won't do.
Anytime we're in discussions with customers or even potential investors, we're honest and clarify, "Here is what we do, here is what we can't do, here's what we won't do, and here is when we plan to do the things we don't do today."

Integrity reflects itself in those small things. For example, you may say, "Oh, yeah, I'll be done in Q3," but you know it's probably going to be more like Q4. If that is the case, you should say Q4. Beginning with the managers and senior leadership, all the way down, we have to ensure that we are staying consistent.

Question: What mechanisms do you have in place to ensure consistency?

As leaders, we definitely want to make sure that people understand that as valuable as we may think you are to the company, or as you may feel you are to the company, if you cross a boundary, if you cross the line from an integrity perspective, then we can't trust you anymore, and you're not going to be working here.

I know mistakes will happen and you need to know what are the things that we won't have mercy for, especially if you break the law or cross ethical boundaries. However, there are other times we remind people about the consequences of a mistake. We make sure people live up to their own consequences. They are not reprieved of those consequences even though there can be alternative paths for forgiveness, so to speak.

You can't have integrity or a lack of integrity in one area of your life and then expect it to show up somewhere else. There is the notion that people are going to make mistakes but like my dad used to always tell me, "There are mistakes you're going to make that you just have to own and that is just as important to integrity as trying to avoid them in the first place."

Question: How does personal integrity show up in your family relations?

Personal integrity permeates every part of my being and shows up in all the roles in my life because you can't expect it to show up in one area and not be in the other. In whatever scenario I find myself, I am always trying to teach. I try not only to teach through showing but also by doing. I also look for ways to create space to have those conversations in the different areas of my life.

One of the things I've learned in life is that common sense is really not all that common, and so it's important, especially for younger people like our kids, to know and recognize what is right because we live in a world where those lines get muddied a lot. There are many people that are willing to tell white lies and cut corners, and in many ways get away with it.

However, that doesn't mean that is okay. So, challenging people to live by a set of principles in every area of their lives is important, and that's truly how you actually live out personal integrity.

CHAPTER 5
Pillar 2: Others First

Small things done with great love will change the world.
—Mother Teresa.

O thers First is probably the most underrated, easy to understand yet hard to comprehend pillar. When we say others first, many of us believe that if we're going to have a successful servant leader organization, we cannot be first all the time. That would be a "no brainer" for us in this process. Yet truly putting another person first takes hard work. It takes being intentional. I define putting others first as creating an environment where each member of your team or organization is treated as a unique individual with intrinsic value that goes beyond their tangible contributions to the organization.

There are a few important keys to this that I believe are really important. First is the idea of creating an "Others First" environment. Mother Teresa modeled this idea, and she is one of my inspirations for this pillar. Mother Teresa has a very famous saying, "Small things done with great love will change the world." If you look at the end of my email tagline, you will actually see these words. This phrase is very important for me because it frames how I desire to interact with people in the workplace, outside the workplace, in my community, and even people whom I haven't yet met. As a leader, you will have to be deliberate about creating an environment where each member of your team's intrinsic value is acknowledged. Just be considerate of the person sitting right in front of you.

When we are thinking about others first, it means we actually stop what we're doing, put our electronics away, close our apps, and shut down the electronics that might keep us from truly interacting with the person in front of us, and look for ways to put that person first.

The way I love talking about this with teams is by reminding people that when someone becomes a part of your team, oftentimes they were hired because of something that they brought to the interview process or a skill set. We hire people for skill but miss the larger contribution they bring to the team. When we treat people as a number—your human asset-they know it. When we treat people solely on the basis of their position, they are aware. I'll tell you right now, they won't stay within the organization for long. Employees are actually people who bring their whole selves to work; not just certain pieces, but all of who they are. I learned this personally by getting an opportunity to spend time at Mother Teresa's home for the destitute and dying in Calcutta, India.

I had the privilege of spending a few days there while studying abroad in my doctoral program. In Calcutta, it is well known that if you are hungry, in need of medical attention and you can't get it, or if you are dying, there is hope in the shadows of Mother Teresa's home for the destitute and dying. The staff when they have beds open; they will go out to the street, grab the next available person, and serve them.

Experiencing Others First in Calcutta

I watched as the Sisters of Charity demonstrated putting others first. I remember one very specific moment where one of the Sisters of Charity took a sponge and dripped drops of water into the mouth of someone who was near death. I was moved and I asked her, "Why are you doing this? Why do you put others first?" Her response was life changing for me. She said, "I want this person to know that they are not alone; I want this person who was dying to die with dignity, to know that they meant something, that they were more than simply a person who was left on the street to die, but that someone actually cared for them." Now, I don't know about you, but that is a life-altering experience.

If I could treat the people that are a part of our team and a part of our organization with that same amount of respect and intensity, that same amount of understanding, love, care and concern, I would be able to truly practice putting others first. I could create an environment where each member of my organization is seen as a unique individual with intrinsic value. Again, I reiterate, what your people bring to your organization is so important; it goes beyond their job functions. Invest in them and put them first, then watch them unlock things within your organization that can change the trajectory of your business. You can be the best version of yourself as you interact with others, and this will be mimicked by your employees. So, what does it look like to put others first?

Application to the Workplace

One of the struggles that many organizational leaders have today is they know about their team, but they don't know their team. There are a few things that begin to rise to the surface if we're going to put others first. We have to genuinely care for the persons in front of us and give that person our undivided attention. When we choose to care for people, we look them in the eye, and we spend time with them.

One of our employees went through a very long six-month period where she lost loved ones to tragic circumstances. She is a diligent worker and was concerned about her work. I told her to prioritize her family, which removed the burden of maintaining a stoic professional persona. She needed to grieve with her people; sometimes, you have to throw a flag on the play (pardon the football reference). That simple gesture was pivotal for her because she felt *seen and understood* as a person, not just a worker. Some would say, that took *super vision*. For context, if you are the CEO of a small company, it would be easier to have more face-to-face contact with your team to determine their spoken and unspoken needs in a timely fashion.

The CEO who presides over hundreds of persons, must ensure that his servant leadership model is replicated by the core management staff. In doing so, they would make decisions like the one demonstrated above. Here's another example: A team member (Sam) was experiencing personal hardships. He asked for two days off to address those issues but was denied. His direct report said **his role** was too important to the company to let him go for the few days. He goes back to his office, thinks about their exchange, then writes his resignation letter. His boss was correct. Sam was the linchpin of their modest operation and his departure cost them millions in revenue. Even worse, he was quickly hired by a competing firm. At his interview, when asked why he left his job, he told them his dad was dying but his boss refused him time off to go see him. His old boss tried to court him back with a bump in salary and a few perks. Sam refused saying, "You didn't even ask me what happened. I realized then that you didn't care enough to ask."

Another way in which we put others first is to believe in their abilities. This is best demonstrated when we delegate duties to them, give them opportunities to grow, and look for ways to help them be the best version of themselves. We are communicating that we believe they have what it takes to be successful and will add value to the organization. Delegating and giving opportunities validates an employee. When we find ways to bring people's voices into the conversation, we learn a lot about how we engage with others; this is another way of putting others first. We exude hope, and we help our team be the best version of themselves. We can see that there is hope when an organization has a clear vision of where it is going and how we're going to get there.

One of the struggles that keeps us from putting others first is our own self-interest. There is an old cliché which says there is no 'I' in team; but there is 'Me', isn't there? Looking out for number one doesn't leave much room for anyone else's thoughts, contributions, or concerns, no matter how legitimate they are. Putting others first– or getting out of your own way- is a very deliberate action; it's not innate. Giving team members an ear and a seat at the table, will not only turn you a profit, but lessen your leadership load and allow your teams to grow professionally and develop psychology.

People are More Important Than Processes

I've seen this happen too many times in organizations, where the importance of work processes overshadows the workers. Have you ever heard statements like, "That's how things are done around here," or "Don't rock the boat." These are commonplace in a process-driven company. It's not the organization that makes the team successful, it's the team that makes the organization successful. In putting others first, in doing small things with great love, we value our employees, we value our team, and when we do that, we send the message that your staff/team/employees are the most important thing, and if you are taken care of and valued by the organization, the organization will grow, and people will be successful.

In the manufacturing industry, assembly-line work is governed by processes because they literally save lives and limbs. There are warning signs, safety protocols and shift obligations that must be adhered to in order to feed a continuous product line. Long before OSHA (the Occupational Safety and Health Administration founded 1971 is a large regulatory agency of the US Department of Labor), workers sustained injuries on these assembly lines because not all processes were beneficial to them. Workers suffered back, hand and neck problems, to name a few, primarily because their equipment was not fitted to them.

In those days, the general sentiment was workers followed instructions and complained amongst themselves. In Japan, they have bridged the gap between management's processes and people's water cooler banter. Their philosophy of "continuous improvement" or Kaizen did just that. Leaders allow workers to adjust their functions, improve efficiency, logistics, even retrofit their workspaces. This philosophy goes all the way up the chain to the CEO. The success of this model is unquestionable since of their most successful manufacturing company, Toyota, is governed by it.

There is an organization with which I work that hires specifically based on this principle of putting people first. They hire for "people fit" over "skill fit." They believe that within their organization, they can teach people almost any part of what they do, but they can't necessarily hire for the people fit. The most important function they look for when hiring they try to zero in on character traits. Example: all across the USA, there is a dearth of skilled labor; we're talking tradesmen like plumbers, welders, and roofers. Metal fabricators and general contractors are actually training persons to fill these needed jobs. But many of them complain that people aren't willing to put in the sweat equity. They show up out of a need to earn but seldom complete their training. Some say they have simply lost the will to work! Can you imagine not having the basic trait of being *prepared* to do something?

Others First Team Activity

When consulting with teams, I do an activity using this principle called *Broken Squares*. It's a very simple activity. You give five people five envelopes with five pieces to a puzzle. This gives a total of 15 pieces, but some envelopes have two pieces, some envelopes have three pieces, and some envelopes have four pieces. The idea is they have to put together a square in front of them so that there are five identical shaped squares.

You would think that's fairly simple, except for the rules. You must do it in silence. You can't gesture with your eyes; you can't point; you can't grab people's squares and make their square for them. What you do is you give pieces of your square away until everyone has had the opportunity to build their own square.

Inevitably, what happens is someone has the right pieces within their envelope to build a square, but the problem is those pieces are pieces that other people need. Their squares will not be finished and in leadership, sometimes this happens. We have to give ourselves away to others. We put others first in the process and when we give the pieces of ourselves, or our leadership away, then what begins to happen is people then begin to flourish, and our organization as a whole, will be successful. Servant leaders always look at the bigger picture.

This activity is always great for debriefing. I will notice that someone has all the pieces that others need. I'll give this hint "You might be the problem," and that usually gets people chuckling and thinking. They will be putting the puzzles together, and then I'll say, "All of you should have the same number of pieces to make your squares." Those two prompts are usually helpful for folks because at that moment, they're able to recognize that they actually might be the problem, or that they need to actually give some of their pieces away, thereby putting others first. When we make that distinction of putting others first, that is when our organizations become much more successful.

THE PRACTITIONER'S PERSPECTIVE

PILLAR 2: OTHERS FIRST

JASON DEMKE
Chief Operating Officer

Practitioner's Profile and Their Organization

Jason Demke is the Chief Operating Officer of a community hospital within a large healthcare organization. His industry is hospitals and healthcare. His work touches every area except for the accounting (payer) side. The hospital he leads belongs to a nationwide healthcare organization that represents the best presence in almost every state of the US except for the Upper Midwest, where it is not so present.

Note: The question of "Others First" was addressed against the backdrop of the COVID-19 pandemic and his industry being a first responder, as well as his leadership from an administration perspective and one who has to interact with the rest of the staff.

Question: What are your thoughts on the concept of putting others first?

As the C.O.O, I have a team of directors. Each of those directors has a team of supervisors or assistant directors and so on and so forth. It is good to be present and be out with the teams, but I spend most of my time with those directors. Therefore, when I think about putting others first, my resume says something along the lines of being an energetic and enthusiastic leader. That is achieved by putting out there what I'm driven by.

However, what gets me out of bed each day is seeing my directors thrive, getting measurable results and getting excited behind it. When they're excited about it and they're having success, to me, that's the most rewarding part of my job. So, when I think about putting others first, I think about my directors.

What does success look like for them? What does it look like for the organization? What are their career goals? Where do my directors want to end up, and how can I help them to get there? How can I help them achieve their best, and what barriers can I eliminate? How can I set them up for success? There is something I've noticed. If I've got a good group of directors, or even an individual who is thriving and growing, I'm thinking, "Okay, what's their next step? What does their future job look like?

Where do they want to be in five years?" If the directors are achieving, the organization is almost always subsequently successful. It's hard to have achieving, successful, promotable people, and not also see your organization achieving and successful.

There is a personal component in healthcare. It can be burdensome. Sometimes you don't know what you're going to walk into each day. You can have a tragic incident in the ER or you can have an angry physician or some sort of catastrophe or disaster. There is almost never a disaster that doesn't impact hospitals in one way or another. Hospital employees have personal lives, with their own personal burdens; yet they come to work every day. They show up.

When I put others first, I'm seeing people and meeting them where they are. I'm recognizing that they are people, not widgets in this big cog where they can get lost. They have interests, they have hobbies; they have children or grandchildren. Making those personal connections with them and seeing them where they are is another way, I try to put others first.

I think bringing that human element helps employees recognize authentic leadership. It shows that I'm interested in you. The results are what they are and we're going to execute on strategies and provide the best patient care possible, but I'm also interested in you as a person. I recognize and see where you are as a person, as a human.

So, it's kind of two different approaches: One is more about career growth, development, the success of the individual in the organization, and how I help them to achieve that as a leader. The other piece is really just that of more human connection, recognizing people are individuals. Let's keep perspective. We get so caught up in the day-to-day grind that we forget that we're people; we have lives; let's get to know each other and reflect a little bit.

Question: Can you provide examples of how your team was putting others first in the last 18 months of the pandemic?

Yes. One of the founders of our company said that bricks and mortar don't make hospitals, people do. If you take away the institution, the infrastructure, and all the things we measure and run after, you've got the people. For us right here in our hospital, it's much more of a community feel than any hospital I've ever been in.

I think a lot of it has to do with the culture that was here before I got here and it has been self-perpetuating because we've got the right leaders, and the right CEO, who is fostering that. People share their lives together outside of work, and they are there for each other. That's it.

I think that simple action and empathy did more in terms of healing and comfort than anything else that could have been said. The charge nurse met my friend's wife where she was.

When I think of examples of people who put others first during the pandemic, I can characterize it with an experience that I had last fall. I had a good friend who ended up here in this hospital with COVID-19 and got really sick. He was in our ICU, and at one point, I was in a meeting on the first floor, when I received a text message from his wife essentially saying, "I'm on my way and so are the kids. They're going to remove him from his ventilator, and I don't know what to do next." I didn't know what to do next either.

I'm thinking, "oh my gosh, she's going to lose her husband and her husband is going to pass away with young kids (teenagers)." I remember asking my Chief Nursing Officer, "What's next? What do I do? How do you know what to do?" More like I was thinking of logistics, right? What can we do to provide comfort? What can we do to make this as easy as possible? I went up to the ICU to be there with the family and I'm sitting there racking my brain thinking, "What do I say? How do I try to show empathy?

I mean it's not hard to be sympathetic in that situation. There were many tears shed. It was heart-wrenching. I'm thinking, "What do I even say to my friend's wife, and the kids?" As I'm thinking through this, our phenomenal Charge Nurse just grabbed my friend's wife by her shoulders. All she said was, "This sucks! COVID sucks," Then she just held her, and they cried together.

More than any words or infrastructure or snacks or anything could have helped, she was just there with her. I think that pretty well sums up putting others' needs first: seeing another person as a human and mourning with them. I've been able to follow up with that family. I know that Charge Nurse made a difference. If I could paint an example of putting others first, then I think that's a pretty good one.

CHAPTER 6
Pillar 3: Communicates Effectively and Listens Well

No one ever listened their way out of a job.
—Calvin Coolidge, 30th President of the USA (1923-1929)

A woman shared that in the first lecture of her master's program, she used the coffee break to look up all the words and phrases the professor used that she didn't understand. At the postgraduate level, it is expected that everyone in the room is highly intelligent. She didn't wish to stick her hand up and say, "Excuse me professor, could you explain that last statement?" Like her, would you pretend to understand and suffer in silence? How long could you keep that up? As the professor, could he discern that his audience had no idea about what he was talking about? I guess he would get a clue after grading their first papers.

Prior to writing this book, communication and listening well were presented as two separate pillars, however in doing research for this book, I realized that we truly can't communicate well, if we don't include listening to the cycle. Communication without listening is simply talking. In the example above, it gets even worse, talking over peoples' heads. Things could even get offensive when we talk-down to people. That one is self-explanatory. As a servant leader, if you had successfully established the previous pillar (putting people first), you would be able to pitch your communication skills with some precision to disparate teams and/or individuals under your charge. Your listening skills would have been honed long before you open your mouth or dispatch an email to communicate with your team.

A good communicator shares thoughts, instructions, and feelings with clarity in a way that people within earshot can understand the message being sent. A clear message is then communicated effectively between sender and receiver. It is communication that leads to the ability to clearly convey the direction or the vision of the organization. One of the most important aspects of communication is knowing the team's strengths, weaknesses, and how they want to receive my instructions.

I heard of a tragic situation where a team member's father died. She was at lunch when the call came, and her coworker wrote the awful news on a post-it and stuck to her computer screen. Needless to say, that work environment is the antithesis of servant leadership. It lacked basic humanity, decency and dignity, things already covered in the first two pillars in previous chapters of this book.

I like the quote by George Bernard Shaw, where he says, "The single biggest problem in communication is the illusion that it has taken place." We've all been guilty of walking out of a meeting and thinking that we clearly communicated the direction in which we were going; the next steps, and what we were supposed to do or how we were supposed to do it; only to be frustrated in the next meeting, to find out your message 'got lost in translation' or got misunderstood by the people that were meant to action them.

There are several factors at play here, provided you are speaking the same language. The famous final words toward the end of any work meeting are, "Any questions?" Having sat through a long meeting, the last thing members want, including the speaker, is a member asking a question to prolong an already exhaustive meeting.

The glares alone would keep that query stuck in your throat. Another factor is how amenable you are as a leader to questions/opinions/comments about a directive you have given. If workers don't feel safe to raise their hand and give feedback, they will keep their mouth shut. Members who like to ridicule others for sharing in a meeting setting are also a factor impeding good communication. People will clam up if they feel they will be embarrassed.

As a good servant leader, you and your core team must be sensitive to these issues. That is the struggle of good communication. If we are truly going to be servant leaders, we must communicate with intention and listen to find where we might be missing it.

Listening well is a learned discipline that is more than hearing; it is about being receptive to what others have to say, even if you disagree. It's not simply just waiting for the moment when they take a breath, so we can start talking again. Take a moment to truly understand what it is that person is saying. Try not to suck all the oxygen from the room. This takes humility, not hubris.

Nelson Mandela, former president of South Africa, gained the reputation of being the last to speak in official meetings. He was a master of listening as others aired their views. How else could he learn of their intent? It is instructive that one of the greats of our age used patience and humility to guide his decisions and lead his country out of an unjust reality. Surely, we can steer our companies using the same methods.

The Art of Communicating Clearly and Listening Well

There are some behaviors that begin to emerge when we elevate listening to an art form. These include the ability to focus. How do you focus when someone is talking to you? What do you do to eliminate the distractions that keep you from truly being present when someone is communicating with you? Communication is always a "two-way street", which involves the listening portion. So, how do you focus? What are the things that you do to successfully focus on the person that is right in front of you? Focusing also includes knowing when to lean into empathy. It is knowing when to lean in to say I'm seeking to truly understand what it is that you're feeling. Focusing is seeking to step into that space and not just empathize, but to really understand what is troubling the person by asking, "how can I help? What can I do for you to be successful?"

As I shared earlier, one of my tag lines is a quote from Mother Teresa: "small things done with great love." The second tagline at the bottom of every one of my emails is "no one ever listened their way out of a job." It is very important for us to recognize that if we are going to be servant leaders, we must clearly communicate the big picture, and we must listen well to the response of those with whom we are communicating.

There is a great deal of communication that occurs daily. According to a communications study from the University of Missouri, Columbia, 45% of our day, that is almost half of our day is really spent listening. If we're really going to step into that space of engaging others, then we have to recognize that a large portion of our day is spent listening. 30% of our day is spent speaking, so truly, as has been said, "we have two ears and one mouth for a reason." We should listen twice as much as we speak.

Be mindful of how you share your message. Oftentimes, leaders are asked for their opinion on certain matters, and they give it like a sage on a stage without asking the receiver follow up questions for clarity or understanding. You run the risk of disempowering the receiver who is listening for a solution to the problem. In short, did you answer what was asked? Have you only been communicating instructions, or have you engaged in meaningful conversation? Our responsibility as leaders is to challenge that person to learn to ask good probing questions.

I coach many executives on the finer points of communicating clearly with each other and their teams. We tend to disempower our teams by solving their problems for them, rather than giving them the opportunity to engage with and learn from the art of asking and answering good questions. If it were easy, communication would be a little more than stringing sentences together. But meaningful communication, that must be practiced, allows servant leaders to get better at asking the right questions and growing in our own understanding of what it looks like to develop as leaders. We learn to ask good questions as we learn to listen well.

Communication and Listening Activities

What Shapes You - Wordless Communication.

I am indebted to my good friend and mentor, Ron Price, for one of the communication activities that I do with clients. Teammates are asked to answer five questions using pictures alone. The five questions are:

- *Tell us about person or event that has shaped your values.*
- *If you could choose another career, what would you choose?*
- *What do you like to do when you're not at work?*
- *How do people work with you best?*
- *What was a significant challenge you faced as a child that still influences you today?*

After the expected protest about drawing capabilities, teammates are put in small groups where they explain to one another the images they have drawn. This not only allows them to practice communicating, but it also allows those that are listening to practice active listening and asking useful questions. Now, these aren't easy questions to answer using questionable artwork. This is done deliberately to challenge people to dig deep.

We recognize that people who shape us at a young age are valuable. It is helpful for us to communicate how those values have shaped us. Talking about those events that have shaped us is invaluable. When we talk about how people best work with us and we can communicate that clearly, that becomes very valuable.

The struggle with communication is the desire to give advice when someone asks us a question. One of the biggest struggles is to say, "well, let me tell you," and we launch into a story. Now to be fair, sometimes that's what people want. They come to you because they trust you. They look up to you; they believe in you, and they want your advice. However, sometimes, advice actually disempowers. On the other hand, if we can help people learn to communicate clearly what they are really asking; if we ask good questions of them, then we're actually developing people who ask good questions; who engage with others, and who are going to, in turn, challenge others by asking good questions in the process.

Active Listening - Mind Wandering

How do you help people understand the power of listening? In my consultancy, we do a fun activity where we actually have participants draw what someone else is explaining to them. For their first attempt, they don't share with others what they have drawn. We use pictures of animals, simple flowers, and things of that nature. Each pairing is given a sheet of paper with the instructions to lead their team in creating this image.

You (the leader) are going to communicate with them and they're going to practice listening. While this is happening, I do a quick activity where I take half the group out into the hall and tell them: "You are going to practice active listening for the next two minutes. All you're going to do is listen. Listen intently to what the other person is saying to you, and every time your mind starts to wander just a little, I want you to raise your hand and then put it down."

The mind is an uncanny thing. It goes on walkabouts without a moments' notice. Before the advent of social media, one could spend half the day reading a good book and the other half daydreaming. Often our minds go for a walkabout in the middle of a college class or at a particularly long stoplight. That last example is particularly jarring when people start honking their horns because you were so far gone, you didn't even notice you now have the green light.

In a professional setting, leaders (servant or otherwise) must train the mind. Being scatterbrained is a bad look for you, your team, and the company image. People can tell when you have tuned them out. They could be talking about their dog getting spayed, and you immediately start thinking about your dog from your childhood and how cute he was. Before you know it, you've missed half of what was said. When you practice listening, I want you to try to be as intentional as possible.

After this activity, the participants return to the room and I'll say, "Now, the rest of you are going to talk to your partner for two minutes about anything you want. They are just going to practice listening. Any mundane topic will do."

Inevitably, what starts happening throughout the room is, people's hands start going up. The communicator (the person speaking) would be the first to ask, "Do you have a question?" The listener will just shake their head negatively, and the activity resumes. At the end of the exercise, those who went out in the hall will explain why I had them raise their hand. Alarmed, the speakers often asked, "Was I that boring?" The truth is, it is really hard for us to listen well, just as hard as it is to communicate effectively.

Part of the problem is that we are able to take in more words than the speaker can utter in one minute. Instinctively, our minds begin to fill in the blanks, much like the suggested typing feature in emails these days. If we are going to be truly good servant leaders, we must learn to just be in that moment. Listen to understand, not to reply.

Regarding the drawing activity, the participants rejoin their groups and lead their team in drawing an image. I indicate that the image be as close as possible to the one that they have in front of them. They cannot explain the drawing but may direct them in drawing it. Inevitably, people get fairly close with the flower and other things. We then discuss how listening affects that exercise. Participants are allowed to ask questions.

The second time around, participants are told ahead of time to draw a different image, but this time they may share information with the rest of their team. What's interesting is the speed with which persons draw once told what to do. Persons will start to draw a rose, for instance, but it may not be like the specimen before them. This is because the key to communicating and listening well is perception. In our minds, we already have a perception of how a flower is supposed to look. Perception is really important.

To put a finer point on it, I display a picture with two people standing next to a number. One of the participants will say the number is a 6 while the other will say it's a 9. It is interesting how our perception plays a role in how we listen or don't listen. When an employee tells his leader about a problem, don't be dismissive or preemptive about it; especially if you experienced it before. Just listen closely before you offer the same solution you had applied previously. Think about it. If you had fixed it properly previously, it really shouldn't be recurring. Did you ask the employee if they had possible solutions to the problem. This is empowering for an employee. A servant leader demonstrates humility by presenting old solution and invites the employee to critique why it didn't take.

Empowering Teams to Communicate and Listen Effectively

In my first book, *Empower. Promote. Launch [Repeat]*, I wrote about what I call the **CORE**. It's an acronym for being **Collaborative,** having clear **Objectives, Raising** up those within your organization and **Empowering** members. Part of communicating and listening well is empowering our team and helping them understand the importance of truly listening well.

We must identify the things that keep us from listening well. For example, you may have had the experience of an unproductive meeting. The next time you go back into that meeting, you may be a little cautious, wondering if this is going to be another bad meeting.

Chances are, when you see that meeting come up again on your calendar, you will create an enemy image in your mind that this meeting is going to go like the last two meetings. When we do that, this becomes an enemy of truly listening well, because we have already created in our mind a picture of how the meeting will go, and what the results are going to be. If we're truly going to communicate effectively and listen well, then we must battle that tendency to label a situation and create these enemy images in our mind that keep us from truly being present to communicate effectively and listen well.

This pillar is an important pillar if we are truly going to be servant leaders because as we engage with others, it will make or break our team if we do not clearly communicate the vision. If we do not clearly communicate the direction in which we're going, and if we do not clearly communicate our expectations for the team and the organization, we will have all sorts of landmines to navigate as leaders. Likewise, if we do not listen well to our team members, they will feel disempowered. I hope that as you continue to develop your servant leader understanding, that you see the importance of communicating effectively and listening well and build teams that do the same.

THE PRACTITIONER'S PERSPECTIVE

PILLAR 3: COMMUNICATES EFFECTIVELY AND LISTENS WELL

DR. HEIDI REEDER
Professor at Boise State University

Practitioner's Profile and Their Organization

Dr. Heidi Reeder is a professor at Boise State University, and the Director of the Leadership Certificate program that's housed in the School of Public Service. Prior to that, she was a professor of communication for many years. Dr. Reeder has a Bachelor of Science degree in communication, a Master's in Communication, and a PhD in communication. Her specialty is human/personal communication, and later that developed into a greater emphasis in organizational communication.

Dr. Reeder has not only studied communication but practices it while working with students, faculty, and others. She truly knows the importance of being a clear communicator from an academic, as well as the experiential, perspective. Personal communication is meaningful to Dr. Reeder because, in her words, "we've got to keep the person at the forefront when you are talking about organizational communication."

Dr. Reeder found it beneficial to do research on relationships, friendships and families, and what communication looks like in an organization. She believes many of those same practices of relating to family and friends can be applied to the organization because of the need to belong. People have a need to be included in their communities, and work is a big part of our community. Here is what Dr. Reeder had to say on the importance of clear communication.

Question: How important is clear communication?

Communication is always creating two things. It's creating the content —the data or the information that I hope will accomplish something, and it's creating the relationship. For example, if I say, "Pass the mustard," it's clear that I want to receive the table condiment, but what is also coming through, although more subtly, is how I feel about you or the kind of relationship I want us to have. At the least, I'm communicating that I have the right to tell you to do something for me.

Let's say instead I say, "Can you please pass the salt?" The content message is exactly the same—send the condiment my way—but due to how I phrased it, the relationship message is different. "Can you please" indicates a relationship that relies on equality or politeness, or perhaps formality, in a way that "pass the mustard" all on its own does not.

I think what people often miss is, they try to be really clear about the content of their message but don't consider what the message is saying about the relationship. Clarity on both of those levels is important. During communication, you're always creating outcomes in terms of things being accomplished—in the workplace, in our neighborhoods, in our communities—but you're also creating relationships through that same communication.

In a one-on-one with me, your assistant, you may have clearly communicated that you want this report done tomorrow, but you may also have inadvertently clearly communicated that you don't believe in me and that you think I'm a lower-level human. So, did we really get what we want, long-term in that case?

Is there a way to clearly communicate that this report needs to be done tomorrow and clearly communicate that I value you and I want to work with you to make this happen? The answer is yes, but it takes mindfulness and practice.

Question: How do you know when you have communicated well?

The reality, as far as I can see it, is that you don't ever really know 100% whether you have communicated well. This is because there's so much meaning going on inside every person. I think what can happen is that we can have a moment where we're both getting a lot of meaning and we can both walk away going "wow, we really gelled; and we really communicated; we really felt that," but we may not have exactly the same sense of meaning inside of ourselves, and I think that's acceptable.

What I might lean more towards is not how I know when I've communicated effectively, but more like if I'm doing everything that I know to communicate effectively; I've got to trust that I've communicated enough. If we're close enough, with a little bit of a difference, we can go on that.

We can be assured that we're never going to have identical brains but there are times when our meaning is just too far off. Perhaps a better question is, what are the signs that you have not communicated clearly?

A really helpful sign is looking at a person's face, if you can possibly do that. Of course, it is not always possible to look at someone's face when we are communicating with them. But if you can look at someone's face, sometimes people have a funny look on their face, and you just ignore it.

So, I can tell you personally that listening is something that I'm always working on. I go through phases where I think good listening is when I can repeat back what the other person has said and let them know they were heard. And then I go through phases where I think good listening is when I'm completely silent within my head, so that there's no competition with the information I'm getting, and I'm not verbally responding to them. So, I think there are some different ways to be a good listener.

However, what communicating and listening have in common is reception, which speaks to whether I'm absorbing the information. In this case, we have not communicated that this relationship is safe and open and that we can always revisit things if needed.

I think sometimes we are in the listening position but we're getting ready to respond, and so we're really not in the reception position. We are waiting to respond rather than just sitting back and being a receiver. This is a very important skill, and it is also really powerful.

It's really powerful to get clear information. Where I think this has really been shown to be true is when I'm in an interview situation, like we're in right now, or like an interview for a job, or on a podcast or something like that. I've found the only way that I could competently answer an interviewer's question is if I really listened all the way through to what they are saying, and I did not prepare all my answers in advance.

This requires self-trust that when they get done with the question, I'm going to be able to answer, even though I didn't prepare while they were speaking.

CHAPTER 7
Pillar 4: Collaboration

Teamwork is the ability to work together toward a common vision.
The ability to direct individual accomplishments toward organizational
objectives. It is the fuel that allows common people to attain uncommon
results. —Andrew Carnegie

Collaboration is one of the foundational and most important pillars of servant leadership. It allows other people's voices to be a part of the conversation. I define collaboration as inviting and rewarding the contribution of others. In this process, we are looking for ways in which people can be involved; ways in which other people's voices can be incorporated into the conversation. Collaboration recognizes that you are not the only person who is contributing to the conversation. Instead, you're looking for ways to collaborate with others.

Collaboration is an important pillar to me. When done correctly, collaboration is meaningful and helpful. Collaboration is about actually growing and developing your team. It is about helping people recognize that they have a voice and recognizing that the answer is almost always found within the group. Sometimes, it's the individual who brings something up in a meeting that unlocks everything and allows people to suddenly step into the collaborative space. Other times, it's the collective group working on a project together. However, the most significant thing about collaboration is what happens in the midst of the collaborative process. You recognize that it's a place where people can actually grow. I take this really seriously with a role here at the university, and specifically with the team that we have within our department.

In my case here at the university, I often speak to the student-workers I am interviewing about the idea of being involved in the collaborative process because I think the voice of the students is just as important as the director's or of those in leadership positions in the organization. I told the students, "You are going to be paid to come to one meeting per week where I want you to share your voice, because your voice is important." In many ways, collaboration is the way to truly mentor and develop upcoming leaders because this is the space where we allow people's voices to emerge, and as their voices emerge, we can actually help to shape and guide them through the collaborative process.

Collaboration is about providing people with a space within which they can grow. It's creating a space in which people feel like they belong and feel like they are a part of what is happening within the organization. Collaboration is truly about building a team. When you are truly leading a team effectively, and you are thinking about being a servant leader through the lens of collaboration, it is important that you work toward a consensus. What does it look like to think about a consensus? How do you work toward consensus if, as you're collaborating, people are coming at it from different angles and looking at it from different points of view?

A quite interesting fact is that, as you grow, and as you develop your team, and as you work toward consensus with your team, you are developing an ethos. You are developing a context in which your team is going to continue to operate. When you're building your team and you're helping the members to understand how you work toward a consensus, you are also valuing those team members and the strengths that they bring to the team.

In chapter 10, you will learn about continuous team development and how we use different assessments to further develop the strength of your team, looking at that strength-based approach with the appreciative inquiry approach backdrop. To me, collaboration is actually the mark of a true leader, who has engaged and is engaging with the process of seeking to grow and to develop their team. In the collaborative process, you recognize that you are not the only one with the answer.

The enemy, or one of the struggles of collaboration is actually being the bottleneck; being the go-to for everything. This then allows the leader to hold on to knowledge, and thus becoming the actual bottleneck for the team. The team will not grow if the organization is not collaborative. In the top-down approach to leadership, that continues to happen.

In the top-down hierarchical leadership in many organizations, the idea of collaboration is actually a foreign one. Top-down hierarchical leadership points people in the direction that says," go do this." Collaboration says, "What can we do?" Another way of thinking about it is through the lens of "how might we...?" When we think about "how might we?" we're moving towards the idea of seeking other people's input because we realize that we may not have all the answers. Nine times out of ten, you don't have all the answers. Your team has the answers and so finding ways in which you can draw those answers out of people is actually how your team will continue to grow. This also allows people to function in a space in which they are doing their greatest work or have the ability to do their greatest work in the process.

Collaboration Activity

In teaching about collaboration, we incorporate an activity in which we spend some time with people who need to work together on a project where they have to collaborate. Initially, it's a very simple project which requires them to work together to actually balance 12 nails on the head of one nail. The idea is to recognize that within the group is the ability and capacity to solve bigger problems, and to solve complex problems.

Through collaboration, we have the actual ability to solve complex problems by looking at the strengths of each person on the team, valuing their input, challenging them to find their voice, and encouraging them to look for ways to be the best version of themselves. We remind them that their voice is important, that every voice matters, and that every voice is important in the process. We do that by building a team, not an empire. Too often, when we think about leadership, we think about building a kingdom. A kingdom is when I focus on what I can get instead of what others need, and instead of building a team. A team, on the other hand, is a group that works together and thinks about others in the process. And we build a team through collaboration. We build a team through working together. We build the team by encouraging other voices to emerge and to be heard; and by allowing others to help solve complex problems, because in the midst of collaboration, you can actually do truly amazing things.

THE PRACTITIONER'S PERSPECTIVE

PILLAR 4: COLLABORATION

MITCH MINNETTE & JILL CRYDER
The Nampa Chamber of Commerce

Practitioner's Profile and Their Organization

Mitch Minnette is the CEO of the Nampa Chamber of Commerce. Jill Cryder is the Marketing and Events Director. Jill helps with the events facilitated by Chamber to help businesses connect with each other and with Nampa's programs, including its leadership program. The Nampa Chamber of Commerce is an umbrella for the business community (both for-profit and nonprofit). It interacts with existing businesses that have been around for 50, 75, or 100 plus years that might be long-standing members. The Nampa Chamber helps them to grow and expand their network and collaborate with new businesses that come in.

The Nampa Chamber is the hub for collaboration and networking in the world of business. It gets the opportunity to work with new businesses from the very start. Nampa Chamber serves as the glue that connects the for-profit to nonprofit and vice versa.

Question: What are your perspectives on collaboration?

Mitch: Collaboration is often a buzzword that businesses or individuals just throw out there. If you walked around the streets of Nampa for 30 days, you would be able to see actual tangible collaboration.

These range from partnerships in the business community helping with the delivery of food for the food bank, to events where we do intentional networking, where you need to introduce yourself to somebody, or set up a cup of coffee, or a business meeting.

We call it intentional networking, but collaboration is literally the hub of who we are and what we do. We're able to connect a nonprofit person at the hospital to someone at the school district, or someone at a local college and vice versa. Someone at the college might need someone to come in and teach plumbing or insurance information; whatever it may be, it requires collaboration.

I think Nampa prides itself on collaboration. The Nampa Chamber is very fortunate to be able to say that one of our strengths is collaboration in actual tangible things. For example, tonight we have volunteers showing up at a local nonprofit to help them with a shipment that came in that needs to be turned around quickly. One thing I didn't know prior to working with the Chamber, is that we have access to people and resources. Nampa is one of those still stubborn small towns that prides itself on rolling up its sleeves to say, "we can get it done." Collaboration is huge for us.

Jill: I think I would just add that we're lucky that it happens here on a big scale and on a small scale. It can be some of the larger things that Mitch mentioned or it can be somebody who needs to be connected with the right people to get a new job or something a bit smaller. Collaboration just happens throughout the chamber as it is a hub.

Question: What does a successful collaborative effort look like?

Mitch: At the end of each 30 days, it might look different based on the needs of the community. One of the commendable things about us is, we're not the government and we're not the city. We are independent. This measure of independence allows us to pivot more extensively and to be as innovative as necessary. With the government, we can't work as fast or pivot. We, therefore, use this measure of independence to our advantage. Whether it's the schools that call us for gift baskets for back-to-school for the teachers or businesses that needed masks or things during the COVID-19 pandemic, the Chamber could pivot and respond favorably. Every 30 days takes on a life of its own, but it's fun to look back.

For example, we could say we have a successful collaboration with events and attendance at events probably as a board member. You could call that successful collaboration when there are 300 people at a luncheon or 100 people at a business and breakfast meeting, and so forth and so on. So, events alone could be an indicator of success, but we just use that as the platform to get people together. We hope there are a lot of things going on behind the scenes.

Again, and you (Jeremy) have seen it firsthand with Jill in Leadership Nampa; the collaboration piece behind that, and the partners that help pull that off is just unheard of. It's hard to even understand how important those collaborations and relationships are.

Question: Jill, talk a little about the collaboration piece of Leadership Nampa.

Jill: Half of that program is your leadership development course; the other half of that program is going out into the community.

Right now, I'm in the stage where I'm firing off emails to say, "Hey, our healthcare month is January. Are we going to be able to come to the hospitals this year?"

I just think this community is so great because nobody has yet told me no. Unless they have a scheduling conflict, that's obviously a valid reason for saying no, but I just think that it's the strong partnership that's evolved over the years.

The team here works really well with the community and people recognize that. I think it's also fun to watch the collaboration happen among the students. That is why it's so great. I noticed last year, so much of that was happening on the bus rides—the downtime when we had a minute to sit down, eat together, or ride on the bus together, and people started talking about connections and their needs. It is not just the leaders who are doing or making those connections, the other participants are also doing it among themselves.

Mitch: I didn't know it at the time, but ever since I moved here in 2004, all my experiences have taken me to where I am today. Whenever we talk about collaboration, I always emphasize the fact that relationships matter. Lately, I have come to appreciate how blessed and how fortunate I am personally. Of course, the Chamber also has high regard for relationships, and I try not to take that for granted.

We sometimes get spoiled to the extent that we can literally make a telephone call, or send a text message to the Mayor, Chief of Staff, Chief of Police, Fire Chief, Chief Executive Officer of a hospital, the governor, or the governor's office. Those privileges don't just happen; that's been 20 years in the making.

Our personal lives (Jill and I) collided with all the work that Chamber had done before us, and that sets us up to have those collaborative relationships. At the end of the day, collaboration would be very challenging if we didn't have the relationships to make it work. There is a trust factor. We know they know we're going to deliver, and vice versa.

Question: What do you do when collaboration isn't going well when people aren't collaborating?

Mitch: I would just say I think it happens a lot and if it doesn't fail, it means you're not trying new and innovative things. Therefore, it's okay for us to hit some of those roadblocks. We try to be innovative and try new things. Some of them work out really well. Sometimes, we may or may not continue, so there's the collaboration. It is us just being brave enough to change and pivot and take a lead role.

Then, at other times, it's fun and interesting because, as Jill and I have found out, you end up on other boards, or you're at other events where you're not in charge, and you have to just smile and own what you can own and not take full blame or full credit. When it's your own event, it's easy because you are blamed or you get credit. But when it's your one piece of the puzzle for other community events, sometimes that's challenging for me because it's this collaboration that breaks down. It does not mean it is necessarily bad; it's different than how you would do it, and that's okay. Sometimes that's been hard to learn.

Jill: There are times when the collaboration needs to come to an end, and we need to move on. We're experiencing that right now in one area. It's tough because you don't want to ruin relationships, but complacency doesn't always work and when there are better and bigger things you can be doing, sometimes you have to make decisions that are not popular.

CHAPTER 8
Pillar 5: Leads with the Future in Mind

The only way you can predict the future is to build it.
—Alan Kay, Computer Programmer

In talking about the idea of futuristic thinking, Robert Greenleaf addressed this as an ethical failure if you fail to do so. Greenleaf put it this way, "The failure to foresee may be viewed as an ethical failure. A serious ethical compromise today is sometimes the failure at an earlier date to foresee today and take the right actions when there was freedom to act." The pillar of leading with the future in mind is what some might call foresight. It is the ability to understand lessons from the past, the realities of the present, and the consequences of a decision in the future. It's seeing a big picture, seeing around the corner as some people might say, and seeing into the future. It is that futuristic thinking mindset that many people within leadership tend to forget when it comes to leading a team, that you're responsible not just for the team in the present moment, but you're also responsible for the team as you look out toward the future and what that future looks like.

The concept of leading with the future in mind is the idea that we have the opportunity today when things aren't "on fire", when there are not a lot of huge things happening, to actually think about the future. One of the ways I challenge leaders is for them to actually find focus time. How do you find time to sit down and think not just about your immediate needs that are right in front of you, but about the big picture; about the future; about two, three, five or ten years from now? What does that look like, not just for you as a leader, but for your organization? How might you actually lead and help others be successful with their future personal growth and their development?

The Effects of Leading with the Future in Mind

One of the reasons I put this pillar before *Continuous Team Development* is because I believe that when you are leading with the future in mind, you are helping your team to be successful. You are also helping your team to be successful when you are developing your team, when you're working on team dynamics, or when you're working on a team report. When you lead with the future in mind, you're also helping to develop future leaders within your organization and beyond.

However, one thing to think about with foresight is that you will invest in the development of people who may not stay on your team, especially as you think about the different generations interacting and working together. You may literally be investing in someone who will be a leader in another organization, or perhaps your competitor, at some point. Are you willing to still invest in that person? Are you still willing to develop that person? Continuous team development gives you the opportunity to do that, but foresight is where the work is done. It is where the hard work is done when you think about the future, and what your organization is going to stand for, stand with, and stand behind.

The Eisenhower Matrix

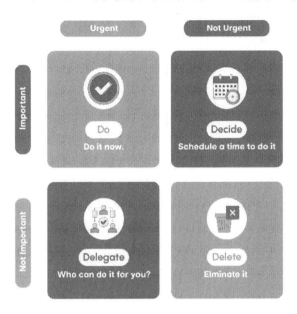

Think about the Eisenhower Matrix. Across the top it has urgent and not urgent, and then along the side has important and not important. These four quadrants help you think about the future, and how you actually would work towards leading with the future in mind. If in quadrant one, it's urgent and important, then you need to do it; you need to step into it, and you need to do it right now; you need to not wait; you need to make it happen.

If it's not urgent but important, that's the box of planning; that's the box that you work towards living in when you are working on leading with the future in mind. It's not urgent, but it's important. This allows you to have a little bit of pressure because it's important but you're not running around putting out "fires". In the third quadrant, it's urgent but not important. If it's urgent but not important, that's where you think about delegation.

Delegating is an important piece to truly leading others, interacting with others, and working with others. With the idea of helping people grow, you ought to think about what to delegate. Now, if you just delegate the things you don't want to do, that's truly not a growth strategy and that's not leading with the future in mind; that's actually just giving busy work to those that are a part of your team and taking things off your plate that you don't want to do. Delegate things that need to be done, but that are not in that important category so, you can actually hand those off to others and they can actually grow in the process.

The last quadrant, number four, is not urgent and not important, and those are the things that you need to rid yourself of; you need to move those things along. As someone who is leading with the future in mind, you want to live in that not urgent but important category. That's a great place to live as a leader who is thinking about the future. This zone allows you to plan and you're not running around putting out the nearest fire in front of you. In this zone, you are living in such a way that you are seeing the pressure of things that are important and you are allowing yourself to have focus time; to find time whether it be once a week, or as you start your day, to actually focus on planning and thinking about the future, so that you don't find yourself a year from now saying, "Oh, I wish I would have... ."

A great example of that for us was the pandemic. As we got into the pandemic, I think many of us on our team thought this wasn't going to be very long. We'll go home for a couple of weeks, and then we'll come back. Well, if we had planned a little better, and had thought a little bit about our future and what that would look like, we would have realized that moving towards or pivoting towards online was actually a great opportunity for us as an organization, because it would have allowed us to widen the footprint of the people that we can reach. For example, other universities were already pivoting before the pandemic towards an online presence, and we (at Boise) did not pivot well at all.

As a matter of fact, we waited too long and by the time we started to move to an online presence, a lot of our competitors had already done great work and were taking students from us because our department did not pivot well. We didn't plan well, and it cost us. It cost us staff, money, energy, and ultimately it cost us the closing of our department, a rebranding, and a new business model that we're now operating, which by the way now includes foresight.

This department is now leading with the future in mind. Our Operations Manager and I meet together weekly to look at numbers and see what is trending; how things are going and we think about the future. We're thinking about how we can make adjustments, not just to price, but from content to delivery methodology. We are now constantly thinking about those things, and we're able to do it because we create space each week to think specifically about the future and to plan for it.

Hindrances to Leading with the Future in Mind

The enemy of leading with the future in mind is the urgent. It is the fire that is right in front of us. Another way to lead with the future in mind is to take that same matrix, the Eisenhower matrix, and just change it just a little bit. My good friend and colleague, Dr. Paul Bentley, showed me how he adapted the Eisenhower model to help organizations think about the future. He Put "time sensitive" across the top and put "missional" along the sides. It is the same thing as important or not important, urgent, not urgent. If you put high time sensitive and low time sensitive, and high mission and low mission across it you can actually start to see how if it's high time sensitive and high mission, then you need to do it.

You need to be decisive about what you're doing; make a decision, step into it, and begin to walk it out. When it comes to low time sensitive but high mission, that's living and leading with the future in mind. That's where you get to design what the future looks like; you get to design what it looks like continuing to move forward, and design living in that space.

The Future Focused Matrix

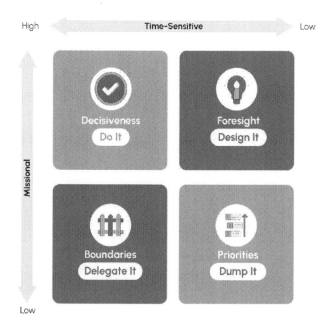

If it's low missional and low time-sensitive, that's where you put some boundaries around it and you begin to think about how to delegate this and what delegation would look like. If it's low time-sensitive, and low mission, that's where you look at your priorities and say, "is this really important? Should I do this, or do I need to move on?"

Allowing yourself to live in that space of leading with the future in mind, can be really helpful in interacting with others on your team because it gives you an opportunity to help set direction and then invite them into that conversation. It's why we put this pillar after collaboration because a collaborator will gather that input and then will think about the future. A collaborator will begin to lead into and live into that in such a way that their team continues to grow and develop. The collaborator also grows and develops. The organization would therefore have a plan of what the growth and development would look like as it begins to move forward.

That idea of leading with the future in mind is about seeing down the road, but not just down the road, but also around the corner. What things could keep us from being successful? What are the things that will help us grow and develop both individually, organizationally, as a team, and as a unit? What will help us as we navigate the future? So, it's seeing down the road, but also seeing around the corner.

One of the things that keeps us from being able to lead with the future in mind, and help our team understand the importance of seeing down the road and around the corner, is that which is urgent. It is the stuff that's happening right in front of us. I call it firefighting. It's putting out the fires that are right in front of us.

We can spend all of our time putting out fires; we can spend days upon days upon days, just dealing with the fires that are right in front of us and oftentimes that's what gets our attention; the tyranny of the urgent, the thing that's right in front of us, the thing that's pressing. It's the email, the text message, the phone call, the boss needs this and needs it right now and we then begin to reshuffle and re-prioritize all of these things and what gets pushed to the side the majority of the time is the action of leading with the future in mind and thinking about the future.

Leading with the Future in Mind Activity

How do we find ways to deal with those things that are in front of us, but not allow them to derail us when we're thinking about the future and we're leading with the future in mind?

There is an activity that I do with a group and one of the things that I often talk about, is how we have to have people who see the big picture, and we have to have people who are near the situation and can give us feedback. Adaptive leadership calls that looking from the balcony and listening from the floor. It is part of the concept of leading with the future in mind. It's being able to see a big picture, and then listen to those who are closest to the situation and how they may need to grow and develop and recognize what that looks like. The activity we do around this is called Zoom, which you have probably seen before. It is a series of pictures that zoom out farther and farther and farther with each picture.

In this activity, I'll hand out these pictures and say, "don't show these pictures to anybody else but I want you to put this in order." After giving this instruction, I'll just let them go. Invariably, what will happen is people who have similar things will start to group up, and eventually you'll have these groups of people walking around and interacting with others. It is not until you have someone who kind of stands up and says, "Hey, I think we have a whole picture here ... I think we're zooming out or zooming in," however they say it, and start to direct it, where you start to see it come together.

What's interesting about that is, it's a perfect example of what leading with the future in mind looks like. Someone has to finally say, "This is the direction in which we're going. This is what we're attempting to do and here are the steps that we're going to take to make that a reality. Now give us your input. What do you see right in front of you?" That's how you can begin to not only debrief this and talk about it but use it as an opportunity to grow and to develop yourself in the process. So, as we look at these different pillars, you can see why it's very important to lead in such a way that allows you to grow and to develop and to be the best version of yourself in the process.

THE PRACTITIONER'S PERSPECTIVE

PILLAR 5: LEADS WITH THE FUTURE IN MIND

RICK MURDOCK & MERRICK MACOMBER
Autovol

Practitioner's Profile and Their Organization

Rick Murdock is the Co-founder and CEO of Autovol, which was established in 2018. Merrick Macomber is the Executive Assistant to the CEO and the Chief Culture Officer of Autovol. Rick wanted to get back into manufacturing and wanted to do it with the latest in technology and use automation and robotics. He wanted to do that because of the backbreaking labor that goes with manual construction and because of the reduction in their labor force and speed.

Rick decided to open a plant with automation robotics because he saw how manufacturing had changed everything from cars to watches. He thought if they could do automation for cars or watches with that intricate type of work, then they could certainly build houses with automation robotics.

Autovol is changing the face of the housing industry. They are the first in the nation to build multi-family housing with robots, automation, and humans inside of a controlled factory environment which is called off-site construction. They are thinking about the future in many ways and developing leaders who think about the future. At the time of writing, Autovol had just promoted nine people from within their organization.

Question: What are your thoughts on the pillar of "Leading with the Future in Mind?"

In the beginning, we just wanted to be the agents of change because we know that right now, in our industry as far as housing, there's no way for the needs to be met using traditional means. We've been doing construction for decades and every year, it falls farther behind. Costs go up and we felt that if we would look to the future with automation robotics, we could get it done easier, quicker, and for fewer dollars.

The other thing was young people. If you look at our industry and you look at traditional construction, young people are not attracted to that anymore. They used to be years ago, but today they're not. Many are not attracted to it because it is too laborious. So, when you go into automation robotics, it attracts a different type of person who wants to be part of automation and robotics and part of a company that does that. In this way, we ended up attracting different people than what we would normally attract through standard means.

Question: How has this direction impacted the company's culture?

I would say that it's impacted our company's culture positively because we have so many different generations of people that are entering the workforce here. With thinking of the future in mind and planning Autovol, we were taking into consideration the longevity of the company and making sure that we were bringing in the youth as well. We were thinking about the factory of the future. Culture played a major role in that because we understand that if we wanted to attract a younger generation to build houses, we would have to attract them via different means and methods.

Culture is a major reason we had in giving people a purpose and a mission that they could stand behind while also having a little bit of flexibility that manufacturing used to not have when it came to the type of environment that we were trying to build. It wasn't about how many hours and how much labor we could get out of a person by working them six days a week. Our focus was on maintaining their health and their mental health for the longevity of the company, and for the future of the company to maintain its growth by keeping a culture of a four-day workweek. We recognized that the younger generations are seeking that high work/life balance.

The important part about the different generations is the education they bring. When we look at our team, you have the older guys who have business savvy. They have run businesses and they understand this particular industry better than most because they have been doing it most of their lives. They are the ones who are familiar with the industry. They have knowledge that they can impart to others.

Then you have this young group to jump in because of automation and robotics. They have knowledge that none of us have based on the internet, their phones, computers, and so forth. They have this kind of education that far exceeds ours. Intergenerational partnership is good for longevity.

We know that we want to continue long past ourselves and others, so we must have young people to mentor and teach how to do what we do and keep the company moving forward. That's why we have a young production manager. In fact, most of our leadership at Autovol is pretty young.

Question: What is the story behind the name "Solutioneer"?

We call our people solutioneers because that's what they are. They are pioneering new ways to build an industry and grow a sector of an industry. They are pioneering every single day, new means and methods to provide a solution of housing and then beyond that, they're always figuring out a solution to possible issues or a better way of doing things.

When we were building the company and trying to establish what our culture would look like, I personally didn't really like saying 'laborer'. Merrick suggested that we call this group Solutioneers and it was agreed on. We also had a wall that said pioneer wall and she kept on thinking of that solutioneer word, and that kind of stuck.

It has created somewhat of a movement. There are other companies that wish that they were solutioneers too, and I would say anybody could be a solutioneer. It is really just a way of being. So, the word solutioneer fits everyone very well at Autovol because that's what we do every day. We find solutions to things that we are having a problem with or things that we don't even know yet.

CHAPTER 9
Pillar 6: Self-Care and Mental Health

The thing that is really hard, and really amazing, is giving up on being perfect and beginning the work of becoming yourself.
—Anna Quindlen

I look at this pillar of *Self-Care and Mental Health* as almost an opportunity for us to have an organizational reset. If you look at this through the lens of generational differences and how generations interact, what's very compelling about this is that within different generations, mental health and self-care is looked at very differently, especially by the older generation. For traditionalists and boomers, mental health was something you didn't talk about. Self-care was something that you did on your own time, and you didn't want to use your vacation time for that, so you didn't do much thinking about self-care.

Each generation engages with the world in different ways. The older generation engaged more with their community and did not talk about things like burnout. They believe you just put your nose to the grindstone and keep moving forward. On the other hand, there's a generation, the Generation Xers and even some of the older millennials, who have been taught to think about mental health, but only after everything else has been completed. You do this after you've finished everything you're working on, then you can consider mental health and begin to put some time into self-care.

Moreover, a younger generation, the younger millennials and Generation Z, look and think very differently about mental health. They think it's a priority, and they prioritize taking care of themselves. They prioritize weekends; they prioritize experiences; they prioritize slowing down; they prioritize taking time. If we are truly going to be servant leaders, then we have to find the space within our lives to make sure that we are helping our teams to be successful.

One of the ways that happens is literally asking your team from time to time, "how are you doing? Are you taking time for yourself? Have you taken time away right now? Have you had a vacation? When was the last time you had a vacation? How are you doing mentally? Are you tired? Are you exhausted? Are you fresh? Are you ready to go?" It's in asking those questions that we begin to build teams that show up and can be the best version of themselves, and we do that by recognizing that self-care, slowing down, and taking care of ourselves is of utmost importance.

The pillar of self-care and mental health is actually one of the highest priorities for a leader who cares about their team. If we are to lead effectively, we must first think about our own personal self-care—how we take care of ourselves, but also the self-care and mental health of those who are a part of our teams.

When we think about mental health and all things that are happening within our organizations, as leaders, it is our responsibility to help our organizations feel supported as they think about their own mental health. Mental health is really important, and it's something that everyone needs to be aware of. It is something that is connected to our physical health. When we take care of our health, mentally, it also allows us to have a better connectedness to our friends, families, communities, and places of work.

It is actually part of being human. It's complex, it's real, it's all those things, but you know what it's not? It's not a sign of weakness or something to feel shameful about because it's not about feeling good all the time. It's about being ok with not being ok, it's about leaning into the uncomfortable and doing the hard work of working on yourself for yourself. This is one reason I think it's very important for us to think about mental health and well-being as the center of our culture. This is why it is so good to see some organizations giving staff mental health days or partnering with mental health providers to offer counseling or therapy for its staff as the need arises.

My 30-Day Mental Health and Self-Care Detox

I liken the whole idea of mental health and self-care to when you're on an airplane and the flight attendant says, "make sure in the event of an emergency, and the oxygen masks fall from the ceiling, put yours on first before you help somebody else." This pillar is important to me because I want to remove the stigma associated with it. The idea of having to continuously work and not take care of yourself is worn by some persons as some badge of honor.

I'm a byproduct of this overworking. I was one who easily worked 70, 80, and 90 hours per week until I hit a wall. There were some things in my life that led me to a counseling center, and it was in that counseling center as a patient for 30 days that I actually started to realize that I needed to take care of myself, that I needed to find a rhythm that was sustainable for me.

As a matter of fact, I was "successful" in the eyes of the people with whom I was working, but I was a shell of a person. I found myself doing more and more and taking care of myself less and less. I found myself actually far away from the person I wanted to be, because I allowed everybody else's needs to be more important than my own. And in the process of really "unraveling" which is the best way of putting it, I literally fell apart, and found myself in a Counseling

Centre with Renee Hollingshed as one of my counselors. You will hear more from Renee in the Practitioner's Perspective later in this chapter.

It was not just a once-a-week Counseling Center, it was a 30-day inpatient therapy counseling, where I began to deal with things going on inside of me. Part of what happened was that I began to deal with things like mental health and self-care. I didn't know what to do with self-care or how to take care of myself. I knew how-to put-up walls and to keep people out, but I did not know how to take care of myself.

So mental health for me started as a 30-day detox where they took away all of my electronics. I did not have access to my phone or email, or anything connected to the internet. I would spend mornings with Renee and afternoons in group therapy. I would spend evenings having to do homework assignments like reflecting on things from the past, taking walks or going to movies.

I had to actually work on finding what worked for me and taking care of the person I was because who I became was actually destroying me. So, this idea of self-care is very important to me personally. Making time to slow down is personal to me. Renee challenged me with that on several occasions: "What are you doing for you? How are you taking care of you?" I was trained for so long to think taking care of you was selfish, but in all honesty, **if I'm going to lead others effectively, I have to take care of myself.**

I have to find space to make sure that I have what I need to be successful, as a husband, as a father, as a leader, as a director, as a facilitator, as a faculty member, and all of those things stem from how I take care of myself, and from what I do for me in the process. Now I am a huge proponent of mental health and I talk about it consistently with business leaders.

Practicing Proper Self-Care and Mental Health

Part of servant leadership is helping your team find sustainable rhythms to their life, sustainable ways in which they can engage with the work that's being asked of them and their families. The big push right now is for this thing called work-life balance. In the past, it used to be that you worked really hard so that you could stay alive, then that work-life balance began to shift to where you work so that you can live, and then the shift now has become work so that you can experience life.

Now we see in front of us this balance between work and life, finding that balance between work and life in the hybrid world that we live in right now and we're seeing this more and more since the COVID-19 pandemic. The pandemic began to show us that individuals were not willing to stay in jobs that were adversely affecting their mental health and taking from them the ability to clearly engage with the world around them.

The pandemic showed us that we could do a lot of things from our homes. We could do a lot of things from different places, and so people began to move. People begin to change their life rhythms because they were forced to make different decisions, and as we went through this process, we realized that people were not willing to stay in jobs that were negatively impacting their mental health.

Self-care takes on many forms. It can be something as simple as going for a walk. It could be something as simple as taking a bike ride, reading a book, sitting outside, and watching the trees for a little while. The problem is that many of us are so busy that we don't stop and smell the roses. I think many of us are undigested masses of non-reflective experiences. We haven't stopped and thought about those things that we have experienced. Part of good mental health and self-care is reflection. It's learning to reflect; its learning to step into the space of really making sure that our needs are taken care of; it's ensuring that we are actually healthy when we show up to engage with others.

It means we need to go to the movies; we need to go out and enjoy a night out with friends; we need to enjoy a healthy, moderate drink; we need to just enjoy being with people and enjoying being around others. We also need to recognize that for some, self-care and mental health is a regimented routine where they are getting exercise regularly, where they are eating healthy. The understanding of how food affects our body is huge, and as leaders within our teams, we need to be aware of those things both personally and with what is happening within our teams as we navigate this idea of self-care and mental health.

Things that Hinder Self-Care and Mental Health

The inability to say no

As we look at the pillar of self-care and mental health, what are the things that keep us from functioning within that space? Well, for some, it's just literally the inability to say no. When you have an inability to say no, then everything becomes a priority and nothing in turn is truly a priority. The inability to say no leads us to places where we are constantly saying, "yes, I could, or can, do that," and when left unchecked in our lives, we begin to stop taking care of ourselves, and we start trying to please others.

I learned this the hard way in my life. I was consistently and constantly, saying yes to others at the expense of family, at the expense of my wife, and ultimately at the expense of my own mental health. It wasn't until I found myself in a counseling center, that I recognized that my true mental health was based on this idea of learning to say no. I was told this in counseling that *a free no, leads to a free yes.* When you say yes to everything, you by default say no to things that might be important.

I have learned that a free no, and saying no to something, meant that I could say yes to something that I wanted to do. When I think about this as a leader, I think sometimes of my responsibility for my team. If I want to create a servant leader organization, it is to actually say no for the team members. To say, "no, our team doesn't have the capacity right now to handle that or, if you would like us to handle that, how would you like us to prioritize the things with which we are currently involved? Can you help us think through a prioritization that would be helpful for you and for the organization?" In doing so, what we do is create an environment where people can take care of themselves, and where they have the freedom to say no without being judged in the process.

Lack of boundaries

Healthy leaders have good boundaries; healthy teams have good boundaries, and that comes from self-care and mental health. I issue the challenge that you find ways to take care of yourself; to think about how you see the world through the lens of self-care and mental health. Remember, boundaries are you for you, not for others. You set boundaries to protect yourself, your team, and people you care about. One of the greatest lessons I learned about boundaries is that many times, people who want to push your boundaries will not understand your boundaries. However, remember that it's not your job to explain or justify your boundaries to anyone. Your boundaries are your boundaries, period.

Thinking one size fits all

What's interesting is that this isn't a one size fits all approach. As much as these terms are part of the latest fad, we can't simply just have one conversation about self-care and mental health and think everything will be okay. It takes more than that. We can't just say, "What can I do for the next 30 days to change?" What we can do is we can make a concerted effort to keep bringing this up with our team. We can recognize that there are no easy solutions to this idea of self-care and mental health. However, conversation will allow us to start to make headway and see changes. As we start to have continued dialogue, the better off that we will be.

The uncomfortable changes that we need to face within our team culture come through having those uncomfortable conversations. The truth is that uncomfortable conversations are uncomfortable, but the more we make that a priority, the more our team health, self-care and mental health become a priority. We can agree that we're never going to fix all the problems, but we can commit to pursuing them together to come up with the answer.

Charge to Leaders

As leaders, if we're going to build healthy teams, if we're going to build teams that are truly going to make a change in the world, we must be mindful of the self-care and mental health pillar. It starts with us. It starts with our well-being and extends to the well-being of our team members. As leaders, our responsibility is to be mindful of the well-being of our teams. It is our responsibility to ask the related questions, and to create the space within which to have conversations, and to think through the idea of how to create a space where people can be free to wrestle with self-care and mental health and can be free to take care of themselves, which might mean that they call in and say I need a mental health day.

Listen, Boomers and traditionalists, a mental health day is so important that I would challenge you to think about how to use some time to take care of yourself, so that you continue to show up and be the best version of yourself for your sake and that of the younger generation. Let them say, "Thank you for painting a picture of the importance of mental health and self-care and challenging us to find ways to work this into our organizational structure so that we can be the best versions of ourselves in the process. This is what makes a great servant leader organization, and this is what I signed up for."

You want your team to see that you are looking for ways to engage with people in need in ways that will be helpful and meaningful to them; ways to grow them as leaders and as individuals. Allow your team to see that you are seeking to find ways to develop social connections that are going to be meaningful; ways to show empathy and engage others in the process of helping people who are in need. It is important that you, as the leader, encourage people to talk about their problems and things that might be plaguing them; it is important for you to care for, to be interested in those that are a part of our teams and our friends. Encourage the team members to provide support for one another, and that includes offering kindness and compassion when people are struggling, not blaming people when they make a mistake, and being quick to forgive. People do make mistakes, but let's inspire each other to work hard, and when we do those things, we can start to see people begin to grow and be what others need.

I recently saw a picture with a caption that perfectly illustrates this, "Be who you needed when you were younger." I think that's what self-care and mental health awareness really look like for our organizations—to be the person that we needed when we were younger in our lives., to help us be the best version of ourselves.

THE PRACTITIONER'S PERSPECTIVE

PILLAR 6: SELF-CARE AND MENTAL HEALTH

RENEE HOLLINSHED
Licensed Mental Health Counselor and Pastor

Practitioner's Profile and Their Organization

Renee Hollinshed is a certified/qualified mental health counselor, who is currently working towards full licensure in the state of Nevada. She has counseled people from all walks of life. Renee has worked for rural clinics which serve underprivileged individuals, mostly adolescents. She is also an ordained pastor and hosts a bi-monthly support group for women who have either struggled with cancer or are just getting a new diagnosis. The idea is to empower them to advocate for themselves and their medical needs, and support them on their healing journey.

Question: What is mental health?

Mental health is learning how to identify what we're going through and how to overcome it, rather than our actual identity. I would define mental health as something that impairs our cognitive ability to function in our personal, professional, and our social lives. Mental health can encompass many different facets of how we think, feel, and behave, but not our identity. Mental health is just what we're going through. I think that some cultures rationalize not getting help due to such myths as, "I don't want to talk about that; I'm not crazy."

Question: What are your thoughts on mental health and self-care?

I think that self-care is important because many times we run everyone else's race not our own, and when it's time to do something for ourselves, we tend to feel guilty. We tend to feel like we cannot embody the idea of doing something personally and for ourselves, so we focus on the mirror of our lives, that is, we project out what others need, but we never really reflect on our own needs, which is so important. Author Edmund Bourne in his book, The Anxiety and Phobia Workbook, says that needs are not necessary for our survival, but they are necessary for our emotional well-being. We do have needs that can stabilize our emotional, physical, mental, nutritional, and relational lives.

When we engage in self-care, that means we're thinking about ourselves, not in a selfish way, but in a selfless way. We're learning how to meet our own needs, even if that means we get that need met by someone else. But we have to be the one who engages in getting that need met. This is very crucial to self-care and creates balance in our interpersonal relationships.

So, ask yourself, "What do I need?" Maybe I need a walk, maybe I just need to breathe, maybe I need to connect with someone else and sometimes that takes us out of our own comfort zone, or maybe I just need to talk to someone about what I'm going through. I can take a bath or I could go on a bike ride, as long as I'm attending to that need. Self-care is an important step toward a "choosing me" journey.

Question: What about mental health for leaders and their teams?

In order to get someone to follow you, you must be engaged in performing the task for yourself. You've got to be able to be passionate about something that's helping you in order to be the good leader of those who are following you because it is difficult to create a healthy leader who has not learned to follow.

So, I think leadership needs to exemplify healthy mental health and self-care simply because it's when we ask for help that we become empowered for recognizing our needs. Asking for help is not a weakness; it is a strength. We use our voices, even as leaders, to validate the fact that we too have needs. Leaders are leaders, but they didn't just get there. They didn't just arrive at that place of leadership; they were in the place of following. Modeling that to those who are coming behind you based on those whose shoulders you stand makes you a very effective leader.

As leaders, we pour out constantly, but at some point, we need to be poured into. I think that we should use this as a model: the more you pour out to others, the more you will need to be refilled, replenished, and renewed. We have to be careful how much emotional strain we put on our interpersonal relationships (our marriages, our parents, our friends) because they may be ill-equipped to support us emotionally and mentally.

It is important for us to have a support system that consists of trustworthy professionals that can help us download past concerns we may not even recognize we're carrying, which become overwhelming burdens to our emotional, physical, mental, relational, and nutritional lives.

Being able to get into a safe space and share your most intimate feelings with someone is very powerful and healing.

Question: How would you challenge an organization to talk about self-care or mental health?

One of the ways that I think we could challenge an organization is to use some very simplified verbiage that encompasses something that people can relate to, whether visual, audio or both. They can be creative in addressing it. For example, I use a house to demonstrate boundaries, or a car to demonstrate the need to change and get out of the rear-view mirror. I think that there has to be some creativity that creates a platform to discuss mental health and self-care principles with your peers.

Otherwise, if you just call it mental health or self-care, it is like, "Oh my God, you know, here we go..." But if we have a hands-on activity, like just using a mirror to explain an analogy, it can help others identify and embrace the concept. When we face the mirror out, the mirror projects what other people want us to see and be to meet their needs, but if we turn the mirror around, we're able to reflect on who we are, our own self-worth, and not who they want us to be. Find an activity or a way to gauge where the team members are and do that in a creative way to promote mental health and self-care development.

Think about someone who is marketing a new product. They do it in a creative way. For example, someone can open up a box, and they're like, okay, get into a small group and take out the contents of the box and start a discussion of what it would feel like if someone said something demeaning to you in the office, or some other facet of office politics.

What if someone was at the copy machine saying some negative things about a coworker, how would you handle that? We have to understand how our feelings are influenced by our thoughts and perceptions. I like to use the analogy that what we say, we hear; what we hear becomes a thought, and what we think eventually becomes a feeling.

If we don't do anything with those things that we receive from external stimuli, like TV, social media, the radio, or from other people, it becomes a thought that starts to race, and those racing thoughts then become feelings that are electrified on the inside. Bourne says when we are disconnected from our feelings, we breed depression and anxiety. We need to talk about mental health and self-care because people need to become more self-aware of their triggers because other people are not responsible for our feelings, only we are.

Some of us are easily triggered and have no idea of the origin of our thoughts or feelings. Therefore, we have to really be mindful and pay attention to our own bodies because feelings and thoughts give us energy. Bourne says, if we are disconnected from our feelings, we experience fatigue, numbness, lethargy, depression, and eventually blocked feelings become anxiety.

He explains that feelings give us energy and when we're in touch with them, we are more energetic. When we are not in touch with our feelings, we experience physical, mental, and emotional pain that breeds headaches, backaches, depression, anxiety, and other physiological symptoms that interfere with our ability to function.

If we don't have a safe space to reveal the most intimate details with someone trustworthy, we generally take those negative experiences home and start to project our frustrations onto our loved ones, our friends, and our families. Home can become a place that we don't even want to be anymore due to potential arguments and disagreements that stem from our not dealing with our feelings.

We then find ourselves in a precarious situation that's going to exacerbate negativity, and we either explode or push these feelings down more and more, which is called suppression or avoidance. We return to work and the negative environment perpetuates the depression and anxiety, and we wear masks because our true thoughts and feelings cannot be revealed in the work environment.

So, we don masks that create pockets of vulnerability that can lead to deceiving ourselves and others. At this point, ask yourself, "Which mask am I wearing?" If we wear the mask too long, the experts say we become the mask. We must find creative ways to eradicate the myth that mental health is a weakness and strive to get people more engaged and willing to sit down and talk about mental health issues and the importance of self-care because it's an important part of our daily lives. It's how we function in wellness. We're not going to be able to function properly without attending to our personal struggles, which can eventually lead to burnout.

I wrote a booklet on how leaders' burnout from "treadmill leadership," behaviors that lead to comfort zone mentalities, places where things are continuous, but do not grow. The booklet is my collection of discussions that depict the need to disconnect from our external world and attend to our internal one (mental health and self-care).

Most times, we operate in life as though we are a power strip, where our spouses and partners, families, children, jobs, co-workers, and social friends are plugged into us, yet we're not plugged into anything. At the end of the day, we take all this negative energy home and feel lethargic, numb, and tired, hardly able to attend to our own needs.

We must ask ourselves, "What am I plugged into?" because the ability to disconnect reminds you that you are the most important person in your life and loyalty to self must come first. You can't be plugged into self-help audiobooks and social media at the same time, as this becomes a draining multi-task scenario. While you may receive great insight from an audiobook, that information creates a challenge to the psychological energy you give social media, and this overshadows any knowledge worth learning about meeting your own needs.

This is how our negative thoughts and beliefs breed negative feelings that beget negative behaviors and while guilt may rise when you care for yourself, with it comes depression, anxiety, regret, resentment, and so forth. Even if you must wear a mask, don't forget to take it off because you want the real you to stand!

CHAPTER 10
Pillar 7: Continuous Team Development

A corporation is a living organism; it has to continue to shed its skin. Methods have to change. Focus has to change. Values have to change. The sum total of those changes is transformation
—Andrew Grove, former CEO of Intel

O ftentimes, we look at team development as "a one and done" opportunity to do some work with the team and then we move on to what's next. Continuous team development is one of the most important pillars or attributes of developing healthy teams. I have found in the work that I do both with my team at the university and with organizations, that truly developing healthy teams takes time, takes continuous development, and continuous work. It takes being very intentional about what that training looks like.

In my years of consulting and working with organizations, I have found some tools that have been very helpful in the process. These are tools I use consistently. One of these tools is from Target Training International (TTI), which is developed around understanding your team and growing your team and culture.

I have partnered with TTI through Price Associates for many years now and there has been an ongoing, growing relationship between the work that I do in the consultation space, working with teams as well as the university with these assessments and tools that can be very successful. I believe that if you find tools that you can use to develop your team, you should lean into those tools because they will be helpful. I specifically use some tools from TTI that I think are very important.

One TTI tool I use is what's called the TriMetrix DNA which looks at three different sciences around self and leadership. It examines your behaviors, how you engage with others, and looks at your motivators—what motivates you. It also examines your leadership competencies. If you actually go to TTI's website, you'll actually see that the TriMetrix DNA is a psychometric test that is used to evaluate the behavioral tendencies of a person. It's used to predict how an individual behaves on their job, what drives them, and in what they will excel.

The TriMextrix DNA is used in many ways. One that I have found to be most effective is in personal and professional leadership development. It can also be very beneficial for executives going into new leadership roles and for high potential team members in helping with job fit and employee development. The results of a TriMetrix DNA are in the form of a detailed report that helps you understand how the person performs their job. The report includes the D.I.S.C assessment results graph in a list of behaviors and competencies. D.I.S.C is a behavioral assessment. D stands for **D**ominance, I for **I**nfluence, S for **S**teady and C for **C**ompliance.

When I work with teams, I do continuous team development around this idea of first discovering who you are through the D.I.S.C assessment. I choose to use the one through TTI as it is one of the most robust assessments I have seen. We use this tool as a way to help people understand how they handle problems, how they handle people, how they handle pace, and how they handle procedures. It's a way of looking at the world through an understanding of how I engage with others in the workplace. If we're going to develop our teams, with continuous team development being a priority, we have to start with knowing our team. We get to know our team through these types of assessments. The results indicate how I show up and engage with others.

These behaviors are the behaviors that others tend to see when they interact with me as we work together on projects and when I'm stressed. The stress tends to come out in how I engage with others. It also looks at motivators, which is the way in which I am motivated to engage with the world around me, and the TriMetrix DNA ranks you in three different categories.

One category is called your *primary driving forces* and it takes four of these twelve areas and begins to put them together. The second is your *situational driving forces*, which allow you to be situation dependent, and the third type of driving force is your *indifferent driving forces*. This is where the driving forces may not be all that motivating to you. What's so fascinating about this is that you can have people who have very similar D.I.S.C behavioral scores and have very different driving forces scores or motivating factors. We spend time looking at that because understanding what motivates you as a leader and motivates those on your team, can be very helpful as you are looking towards team development and grabbing a hold of what that looks like as you engage with the world around you.

Then we look at the leadership competencies. This, to me, is one of the important pieces to using this assessment because it allows you to see areas that are well developed all the way through areas that could use development. In the process, it allows you to begin to say these are areas where I'd like to grow and develop. Continuous team development is not just about team dynamics; it's also about growing the individual. It is about growing the team members and helping them to be successful beyond the organization. I think that we miss the fact that as we are growing whole people with whole lives in a whole world and, they may move beyond our organization.

This continuous team development through assessment is just one way in which we can develop our teams. One of the goals from these assessments is having sections like checklists for communicating. This allows you to dig deeper into how people want to communicate, or the manner in which they want you to communicate to them, and how they don't want to be communicated with. This is extremely helpful when working in groups or teams because this allows you to clearly identify how people want to connect and communicate within their team. I'm amazed at how many people don't actually have conversations about how to communicate effectively or what is the best way to communicate with each other.

One of the methods we use often is trying *to figure out* routine. This means one may have a co-worker with whom you are trying to figure out how to communicate. You go in and try an approach. If the approach doesn't work, you go back to the rest of the team and say that way didn't work. Then, you try a different way and, by trial and error, you eventually figure out to the best of your ability how this person wants you to communicate with them.

Yet, if we took 15 minutes with this assessment, and we had people share, here are the top two or three ways that I want you to communicate with me. It takes the guesswork out of communication. This is where continuous team development really can change the dynamic of your team because now you are spending time using what you're learning about yourself to help others understand how to work with you and the retention rate goes up in this kind of process.

We also use these assessments, as we're looking at strengths and weaknesses, as we're looking at keys to manage and keys to motivate. These can all be helpful with your team or your organization when you're working with people around this idea of growing the competency of your team and the team dynamics that are at play.

Another assessment that I use when I'm working with teams and organizations is the EQ Assessment or Emotional Intelligence assessment. It looks at five different factors and helps you to understand how you engage with others and gives you opportunities to grow some of those areas within the EQ world.

The five areas of the EQ test are broken into two different sections. You have intrapersonal, which is what's going on inside of you, and interpersonal, which is how you interact with others. The intrapersonal section of the EQ Assessment actually ranks you on self-awareness, self-regulation, and motivation. **Self-awareness** is the ability to recognize and understand your moods, emotions and drives, as well as their effects on others.

Self-regulation is the ability to control or redirect disruptive impulses or moods or the propensity to suspend judgment, to think before acting. **Motivation** is a passion to work for intrinsic reasons that go beyond money or status, a propensity to pursue goals with energy and persistence. Those are the three areas of the intrapersonal section which sees what's going on inside of you, when we use the E Q assessment.

Then we have interpersonal skills which deal with how I interact with others. The interpersonal has two areas: **Social-Awareness,** which also can be empathy, is the ability to understand and relate to the emotional makeup of other people and treating people according to their emotional reactions. The other area is **Social-Regulation**, which is a social skill. This is proficiency in managing interpersonal relationships, and in building interpersonal networks. It is, also, the ability to find common ground and to build rapport with others.

The TriMetrix assessment allows us to look wholistically at an individual and what they contribute to the team. The TriMetrix DNA and the EQ assessment through TTI have both been very instrumental in team development, helping the team grow, but it's not just assessments; it's also learning how to use what we've learned from those assessments to build healthy teams. This is where we can have continuous team development.

The practice of continuous team development is arrived at in recognizing the strengths that each member brings to your team, and harnessing those strengths, using those strengths for the good of the organization, and putting people into places where they will flourish and prosper. That is team development. It is knowing your team, engaging your team, and looking for ways to grow those team members in the process.

Continuous Team Development Activities

In working with teams and organizations, one of the ways that I like to talk about continuous team development is an activity in which I put up two pieces of flip chart paper. Then I split the room in two and say, "those of you over here, give me characteristics of someone who develops people," and on the other side I'll say, "give me some characteristics of someone who drains people."

Then I'll have them switch and go to the other side of the room and it's quickly evident that most of us are very familiar with people who are drainers, but it's a little harder for us to think about people who have developed us. So, the challenge is, if we're going to create an environment where we are increasing our servant leadership ability, we have to think about the idea of how we develop others, what it looks like for us to develop others in the process.

One organization that I'm working with closes every Thursday from 12 to 1:30 to facilitate team development. Sometimes they have just longer staff meetings where they're talking about the organization and the organizational needs. Sometimes they're literally doing team building activities together which includes things like bringing in a facilitator like myself into the organization to do some activities around team building, or actually going out and having a longer lunch together, or going out to places where you can drive go karts together, or to an ax throwing event, or whatever it might be as an opportunity to bring together people to get to know each other and continue to develop their team.

Another organization that I'm working with takes their people in groups of 30 through these assessments over a five-month period, 90 minutes once a month, with 30 people working on team dynamics, team development, and doing some team building activities together.

I have many team building activities that I do when working with teams. We do simple activities like learning to collaborate and balancing 12 nails on the head of one nail. We do activities about giving things such as the broken square activity that we talked about in a previous chapter. I also do activities around team building where teams have to work together on a large project for two hours and solve a problem as a team. The members are then required to use what they've learned in the debrief to grow. We also do some activities around change; helping people navigate change.

The whole purpose of these activities is to facilitate retention within the organization and develop people individually. The activities are a part of professional development and must be continuously done. As a leader, ask yourself what professional development would like for your people. There're so many different opportunities to ensure that your team members are continuously engaged in professional development. If your team works online or does remote work, get creative and see how best you can facilitate team development on an ongoing basis.

At the university, there is a rhythm to our development as a team. There are team check ins, our team huddles, and team building opportunities which keep continuous team development in the forefront of our minds and of our organization. I believe that if we are committed to developing our team that we will retain employees because people want to be a part of something.

When you look at this even from the previous work that I've done around generations, you'll see that though traditionalists oftentimes find themselves leaving the workplace, many of them are in their 80's, they've raised Boomers and boomers look at the world through the lens of collaboration because they've grown up having to share because infrastructure wasn't ready. So, they're consistently already looking for teams, even Gen Xers, who sometimes seem a little bit aloof when it comes to teams, will work with people with whom they feel comfortable and confident working around.

We also have millennials who have grown up working on projects together, and then Generation Z, who is now coming into the workplace; they want to grow both personally and professionally in the workplace. They're looking not necessarily for bosses but mentors. They're looking for people who are going to come alongside and help them grow and develop them in the culture in which we find ourselves.

Enemies of Continuous Team Development

In the day and age in which we find ourselves, I believe that the tool and the pillar that's going to grow effective teams is going to be continuous team development, but what's the enemy of that? What keeps us from doing that? Well, the primary enemy is the one-and-done mentality which says, "I did a team building event once, not everybody showed up, so I'm not going to do it again", or "we have an annual team building event and we leave it at that." Continuous team development takes time, energy, and being intentional.

Here is the other thing; it takes resources. Those resources might be time, team talent, engagement, or even money. But think for just a second about what is the tradeoff, the cost of bringing in a trainer to develop your team, versus the onboarding experience of having to rehire somebody because they don't feel part of a team and they quit. Now you have a vacancy where other people have to pick up the slack. You then have to hire someone else, who may or may not be the right fit and all that goes with hiring someone new.

Every time you have to replace someone in your organization, it's 2.5 times the annual salary of the person you are replacing. This means you can hire many trainers and many facilitators to do team building and team development for the cost of one employee turnover, let alone multiple. So how do you want to grow your team? What does it look like for you to develop people within your team and organization?

In summary, continuous team development both individually and as a team is the key to retention. It is the key to happy employees. It is the key to teams and families that are high performing and accomplishing big things. As you look to the future, I believe this pillar is one of the most important pillars in developing healthy teams. For a summary of these and other activities to practice the seven pillars, see Appendix A on Practicing the Pillars.

THE PRACTITIONER'S PERSPECTIVE

PILLAR 7: CONTINUOUS TEAM DEVELOPMENT

RYAN BAXTER
Owner of Modern Auto Service

Practitioner's Profile and Their Organization

Ryan Baxter is the owner of Modern Auto Service, an Auto Repair Shop in Fruitland, Idaho. He has worked as a technician since 2011. The business has been in operation since 2016. Modern Auto closes its facilities every Thursday for an hour and a half to do team development and team training. At Modern Auto Service, there is a sign that says, "to better serve you, we are closed on Thursdays from noon to 1:30 for staff training."

Question: Tell us more about the Thursday time-out for team development activities.

When we started the business, my mind was flooded with billions of ideas about how to improve the business. I frantically tried to implement them, but I quickly found that we couldn't get past the triage phase. We spent all of our time putting out fires and could never find the time to solve the real challenge of why we have so many fires. Within a month of opening, I realized that spare time is an illusion, and implemented a weekly development meeting with our two employees. We ordered lunch and carved out 90 minutes to work on ourselves and our systems. The topics we covered ranged from technical procedures to soft skills and everything in between.

One of the most memorable training I can remember was focused on how to be more descriptive when communicating. Our team worked in groups of two and took turns describing an image while the other person tried to draw it. It was a cheesy activity but helped us have important conversations.

Question: How have your customers responded to this change?

During those first six months, clients would walk into the office while we were holding training and I would leave our team, run downstairs, and help the client. I knew it was really hindering our training, but could I really close our business in the middle of the day? I didn't know how clients would receive it.

Our team discussed it and decided that if we communicated it well, we could make it work. We updated the business hours on our website and Google. We added a message to our phones that described our Thursday schedule, and we updated our door signs to explain the reason for the change. We had a few hiccups along the way, but for the most part, our clients adapted and were fine with it. As time went on, we found that almost every customer that noticed our training schedule commented positively and commended us.

What I have found through our training experience and various marketing activities is that people really care about people. We provide products and services to our clients and we need to do a good job at that, but what sets us apart and what clients really care about is how we take care of people. Our business doesn't create many "Advertisements" on social media.

You will rarely see us post a coupon or special. What you will see are pictures of people. When our technicians gain a new certification, we celebrate it! When our employee has a work anniversary, we celebrate it! When a client or someone in the community does something meaningful, we praise and promote it. Instead of an "Advertisement" we show that our people matter, and then our clients ... who are people too, assume that we will treat them like they matter.

In 2019, I joined an automotive peer group that totally catalyzed my growth as a leader. I was the youngest member of the group and I was flooded with knowledge and direction from the best shops in the business. Many of the businesses had great systems, clear expectations, and phenomenal performance, but they seemed to burn out their people.

In the auto repair business, cars are always breaking down, and everything is urgent. As I listened to the other owners, I noticed that they were always running at full throttle. They had no consistently planned capacity in their schedule for development. Aside from a few slower months of the year, their staff would come in early, and work late, and if a meeting was needed, it was outside of business hours. I think when employees operate in an environment like that, they begin to feel like the owner values their own time, but not the employee's time ... and when you step back, I think they're right!

Question: Have you seen more employee connectedness and buy-in because of the training?

I won't pretend for a minute that our approach always works. Sometimes we hold training and we bring insignificant things to light and blow them out of proportion and it distracts us from addressing the weightier matters.

We aren't professional trainers and sometimes we go into a meeting thinking we planned something great, only to find we are dead wrong. That being said, our efforts make a difference. The bar is low in the automotive world. If we deliver 75% of what we say, we will still be better than what most people expect.

I absolutely love building a team in this environment where they can really shine. We help our technicians develop confidence in their technical skills and know how to present information in a way that builds trust with clients and co-workers. We help our service advisors become exceptional communicators that can build trust and provide a world-class experience for our clients.

To be honest, not everyone values this kind of touchy-feely stuff. It has even pushed some people away, but the people that have stayed are amazing! Who would have thought that a little bit of time and commitment could not only help us build an amazing team, but it could cultivate a client base that we love to work with!

CONCLUSION
Putting It All Together

If everyone is working together, then success takes care of itself.
—Henry Ford

As a leader, you should be asking yourself, "How do we get better at serving the people that are a part of our organization?" We set out to answer that question in this book with the goal of helping you to increase your servant leadership capacity through serving and influencing your team, rather than telling your team what to do. Our goal has been to encourage you to build a culture of care in organizations where employees thrive instead of feeling burnt out and leaving our organizations in frustration.

In part I of this book, we explored the pitfalls of the traditional leadership model and what makes a good leader. Having analyzed several leadership styles, we proposed the servant leadership model as the best model to build effective teams and successful organizations. In Part II, we explored the seven pillars of servant leadership, and how to build a servant leader organizational culture. As we begin to unpack and look at the ways in which we can begin to practice these pillars and put these pillars into effect, they can actually have a profound impact on our community.

I constantly challenge people to think about how to create owners on their teams. It is one thing to have people who show up for work and then leave, and at least you're happy that they show up for work, but creating owners is a whole different mindset. Think about it as renting a house versus owning a house. When you rent a house, when something breaks or when something doesn't work, you call the owner. You call the property management company, you call the landlord, and you say, "Hey, this is broken."

Sometimes the landlord or property agent says things like, "okay, we'll fix it," and then deduct it from your monthly rent or so on and so forth. However, when you own your home and something breaks, you still have to pay your mortgage and you still have to fix the issue. Now, you still might call someone, at least I know I do. I'm not quite the handyman, so, I would call somebody. However, at the same time, when I own it, I have buy-in to fix it to keep the house looking good.

The same is true when we talk about renters and owners in the workplace. To create owners means you're creating people who have buy-in, people who care about the future of the organization, people who are excited about things that are happening within the company, people who live and breathe and are brought into the vision and direction of an organization. Those that are renters rent their job, they show up; they do what they need to do to receive a paycheck and then they leave, and their world is not connected at all with work. Work is a means to an end, that's it. Renters look at their job as disposable. They can find another one if this one doesn't work. If I don't like my owner, if I don't like my leadership, if I don't like... fill in the blank. So, we challenge organizations to use these pillars to create owners.

Therefore, how do you create people who have bought into the culture of the organization? How do we actually create a culture of putting others first? We can do that by asking, "Are we developing people, or are we draining people?" As developers engage with people around them, they leave them better than how they found them. Drainers leave people worse off than when they first engaged with them. So, the challenge is, how do you create an organization where you're truly putting others first? You do that by developing people; not draining people.

How do we actually think about being better together? I think we're better together when we lead from within. When it starts inside out, where we take our EQ and our IQ and we put them together, we take our heart and our mind and we put them together and we show up and be the best version of ourselves; we equip our team members to do the same. So, we give them opportunities to continuously develop, and then we challenge them with homework assignments, small ones, yes, because we still have jobs to do and no one wants to go back to high school or college, but we challenge them with ways to put together the things that they are learning and begin to lead from within.

The other consideration which is really important in thinking about being better together is trust. Literally, how do I trust people that are part of my team? How do they know that I trust them? How do they know that we're engaged on a journey together? Well, one way is to give them meaningful tasks; delegate meaningful work, collaborate with them, put them first, help them grow, help them be the best version of themselves, and as you do those things, as you lead from within, you are better together; that's the key to walking through all of this.

Truly becoming *a servant leader is much more a state of mind than a set of directions*. You can't just officially go to a class or even read a book and that's all there is to it. It is how you change your mindset. It is about intentionally saying, "I'm going to put others first." Robert Greenleaf was very clear on the idea of consciously choosing to serve first. It is the state of mind that I think challenges us to become a servant leader, so it's not a set of directions.

If you are reading the book or taking a course because you hope to get a checklist of ways to lead, thinking if I do this or that, then I'll be a servant leader, you will miss the mark. In reality, the bigger conversation that we're having is not about a set of directions or a set of steps; it's much more about connecting with, walking with, and understanding your team members, even though this type of leadership is lifelong and ongoing.

You don't arrive as a servant leader. One of the things that always makes me cringe a little bit is when people introduce themselves as, "I am so and so servant leader." I would much rather have someone describe the way I interact with them as servant leadership than to try to describe my style as, "Oh hi, I'm Jeremy, I'm a servant leader." The process of this, though, is very important. My research with focus groups shows that 85% of those who become a leader do so because of the influence of other leaders. They are in a leadership position because someone invested in them in the process. Great leaders are all about reproduction. They reproduce themselves in organizations. They reproduce the culture that they're hoping to see within the organization, and they give themselves away in the process.

At some point, leaders turn around and realize that they have influenced all these others, and the organization has changed and grown and developed, and there's a whole group of other people who are now serving and leading and working with others. Leaders do it through that law of reproduction. In this process, they identify the people that are in need. They prepare those folks through continuous team development, and professional development, and they affirm what they see happening within their team and the process is important.

Servant leadership is much more about purpose than position. I've been convinced from early on that leadership is a lot less about a title, an email tagline, or what the company job description says, and much more about influence and leading others with the influence that we have. The more that I study servant leadership, the more I realize that it's about purpose over position. It's about helping people to understand their purpose; how they connect to what is happening in the world around them or within their organization. It is about connecting people to their passion and purpose and doing it together.

I love the fact that if you step back and you look at servant leadership, you recognize that servant leaders succeed when their followers succeed. It's a very simple way of looking at the world. If you need any sort of process steps, just remember that 1). servant leaders are successful when their followers are successful. 2). Servant leaders listen more than they talk. That's a vitally important reminder for us. I think this is really important. The irony is not missed upon me as a facilitator, a professor, a community leader, and advocate for these programs.

Certainly, **leadership is much more about hearing what others are saying versus trying to command them to speak a certain way.** When we put it all together, it's purpose over position; it's the success of followers over success of myself, and it's listening more than talking.

Practicing the Pillars

Here are some activities you can use to develop a servant leader culture in your organization. Some of these activities were explained in the chapters for the pillars. We have compiled some of them here for easy retrieval and use. Feel free to create your own activities around each pillar.

Pillar 1: Personal Integrity/Behaving Ethically

The Ethics Ball: There are all sorts of questions on the ball and we use that to lead our discussions. For example, there would be questions like: "Is it ever right to tell a white lie? Do you believe in the phrase "finders keepers, losers weepers?"

Instructions: Throw the ball around the room and have people answer the questions on the ethics ball. Use the questions and answers to have a discussion about the issues raised in making ethical decisions and what that looks like as we walk this out.

The X Y Game: Put people in groups and they have to hold their X or Y with a dollar amount attached to their X or Y. The best way for everyone to win is for four teams to hold up their Y, but if three teams hold up a Y, and one team holds an X, then all of the people who held up Y get a negative one dollar. The teams who held up X get plus three dollars.

Results: You may start to see how people will start to turn on each other even in a game like this. This gives us space to discuss personal integrity and ethics in the workplace and what it really looks like for us to engage with others and think about not throwing an X when we are connecting two people that are part of our team, but actually allowing everyone to throw a Y.

Pillar 2: Others First

Broken Squares: This activity is always a great debrief. Participants will complete a puzzle using the pieces of a square that they are given.

Instructions: Give five people five envelopes with five pieces to a puzzle. This gives a total of 15 pieces, but some envelopes have two pieces, some envelopes have three pieces, and some envelopes have four pieces, and the idea is they have to put together a square in front of them so that there are five identical shaped squares.

Rules:
1. Complete the activity in silence
2. Do not gesture to each other for help
3. Do not grab people's squares to make your square
4. Give away pieces of your square until everyone has had an opportunity to build their own square
5. Activity Leader – Start walking around the room to check if someone has all the pieces that others need. Give them a hint that they might be the problem.
6. Remind the group that all of them should have the same number of pieces to make your squares

Lesson: In leadership, sometimes this is what we have to do. We have to give ourselves away to others. We put others first in the process and when we give the pieces of ourselves or our leadership away, then what begins to happen is people then begin to flourish and then your organization will be successful.

Pillar 3: Listens well- Is a Good Communicator.

What Shapes You - The Five Questions

Instructions: Ask your teammates to answer five questions, but they can only answer these questions using pictures, no words are allowed. Your teammates should draw pictures to show their answers to these five questions:

- A person or event that has shaped your values is ...
- If you could choose another career, what would you choose?
- What do you like to do when you're not at work?
- How do people work with you best?
- What was a significant challenge you faced as a child that still influences you today?

In your groups, tell your teammates why you drew what you drew.

Results: This not only allows you to practice communicating, but it also allows those that are listening to practice active listening and asking good questions.

Active Listening - Mind Wandering

Instructions: Take half the group out into the hall and tell them they are going to practice active listening for the next two minutes and all they will do is listen. Listen intently to what the person who is talking is saying to you, and every time that your mind starts to wander just a little, raise your hand and put it down. Be intentional as possible.

After this activity, bring this group back into the room. Tell the rest that they are going to talk to their partner for two minutes about anything they want. They are just going to practice listening so talk about anything; talk about what you had for breakfast this morning, talk about your day yesterday, talk about something from your family; you're just going to talk.

Results: People's hands will start going up and first the people who are talking will say, "do you have a question?" The listener will just shake their head (saying no), and we'll continue the activity.

When they're finished, ask those who went out in the hall to explain why they raised their hand and then have a discussion on active listening and communication.

Pillar 4: Collaboration

Balancing the 12 Nails: Instruct the team to actually balance 12 nails on the head of one nail, and they have to work together to actually do it. The nails cannot touch the wood and must be balanced on the head of the nail sticking out of the wood. Work together to solve this challenge.

Pillar 5: Leads with the Future in Mind

Zoom: This activity is about being able to see a big picture. Show a series of pictures that zoom farther and farther out.

Instructions: Get the book zoom, which has 36 different pictures, each gradually getting further and further out. Hand out these pictures and tell them not to show these pictures to anybody else. Ask the participant to put the pictures in order just talking with one another but not showing each other their pictures.

Result: What will happen is people who have similar things will start to group up, and eventually you'll have these groups of people walking around and interacting with others. It is not until you have someone who kind of stands up and says, "Hey, I think we have a whole picture here … I think we're zooming out or zooming in," however they say it, and start to direct it, where you start to see it come together. Someone has to finally say, "This is the direction we're going. This is what we're attempting to do and here are the steps that we're going to take to make that a reality."

Pillar 6: Self-Care and Mental Health

Team Check-Up Questions: From time to time ask your team these questions:

- How are you doing?
- Are you taking time for yourself?
- Have you taken time away recently?
- Have you had a vacation?
- When was the last time you had a vacation?
- How are you doing mentally?
- Are you tired?

- Are you exhausted?
- Are you fresh?
- Are you ready to go?

Pillar 7: Continuous Team Development

Use these activities to discover things like your team member's personality traits, preferred method of communication, areas of potential conflict and their strengths, how they respond under stress, and identify areas for personal growth and growth as a team.

Energizer vs. Energy Drainer

Instruction: Split the room into two groups. Say to one group, "those of you over here, give me characteristics of someone who develops people." To the other side, say, "give me some characteristics of someone who drains people." Discuss your observations. Very often, it's quickly evident that most of us are very familiar with people who are drainers, but it's a little harder for us to think about people who have developed us.

a. Do the TriMetrix Assessment with your team and discuss the results.

b. Close the organization weekly for 60-90 minutes and do team-building exercises or bring in a facilitator. Go out as a team and do something fun.

c. Try activities like Broken Square or balancing the 12 nails.

d. Do a short-term project together to solve a problem as a team for two hours and then do a debrief.

About the Author

Dr. Jeremy Graves is the Director of Professional and Continuing Education with the Division of Extended Studies at Boise State University. He is First-Year Faculty for the Community Impact Program, a Presidential Initiative of Boise State Universities Dr. Tromp. He teaches leadership classes in the LEAD program and works with organizations around strategy, culture, and Generational Synchronicity.

Jeremy brings almost thirty years of leadership experience into the classroom. He has taught classes, presented workshops, and keynotes on Generations in the Workplace, Generational Diversity, Team Building, EQ, DISC, Servant Leadership, Business and Leadership. His greatest passion is working with multi-generational teams. He specializes in helping organizations discover keys to getting the most out of their generational teams. He excels at organizational development and cultural restructuring.

In May of 2018, he completed his first book entitled *Empower, Promote, Launch Repeat: Create a Culture of Generational Leadership using 4 Core Strategies*. Jeremy is married to his best friend, Stephanie, and they have two boys. They reside in Boise, Idaho, and enjoy spending time with family and friends. Jeremy is also an avid hockey fan and will use just about any excuse to take in a hockey game.

References

Autry, J. (2004). *The servant leader: How to build a creative team, develop great morale, and improve bottom-line performance.* Currency.

Bourne, Edmund J. (2015). *The anxiety and phobia workbook, sixth edition.* New Harbinger Publications.

Brown, B. (2018). *Dare to lead: Brave work. Tough conversations. Whole hearts.* Ebury Digital.

CBS News. (2022, March 2). Melinda French Gates opens up about divorce: "I couldn't trust what we had." Mental Health and Divorce. https://www.cbsnews.com/news/melinda-french-gates-opens-divorce-journey-of-healing/

Clinton, J. R. (2012). *The making of a leader: Recognizing the lessons and stages of leadership development* (2nd ed.). NavPress.

Greenleaf, R.K. (1983). *Servant leadership: A journey into the nature of legitimate power and greatness.* Paulist Pr.

Graves, J. (2018). *Empower, promote, launch [Repeat]: Create a culture of generational leadership using 4 CORE strategies.* Create Space.

Lee, D. (1983, March 03). "Listening: Our Most Used Communication Skill." Communications. University of Missouri Columbia.

https://mospace.umsystem.edu/xmlui/bitstream/handle/103
55/71861/CM150-1983.pdf?sequence=1

McFeely, S. and Ben W. (2019, March 13). This Fixable Problem Costs U.S. Businesses $1 Trillion. Gallup Workplace. http://bit.ly/3IWIMPB .

Tanner, O.C. (2022). *Thriving Cultures*. What kind of company culture do you have? https://bit.ly/3YtJ9qo

Made in United States
Troutdale, OR
09/13/2023

12881510R00094